X
/9

D0630030

Glen Mercer

THE LAST RIDE

By

Former Bullriding Champion

GLEN "PEE WEE" MERCER

With

PATRICK D. SMITH

The Last Ride
by: Glen "Pee Wee" Mercer and Patrick D. Smith

First Edition

Published by:
Sea Bird Publishing, Inc. – 218 Ash Street – Melbourne, Florida 32904
321-727-0801 – email: jculber@grafixnpix.com
Copyright© 2000

Mike Rastelli Photographs Copyright©. Permission to reproduce generously granted by Mike Rastelli. Continuous tone prints are available upon request by contacting Mike Rastelli, 11760 S.W. 38th St., Ocala, FL 34481-1317, 352-629-4458.

Publisher's Cataloging in Publication Data
Mercer, Glen "Pee Wee" with
Smith, Patrick D.
The Last Ride/by
Glenn "Pee Wee" Mercer with Patrick D. Smith – First Edition
ISBN 1-886916-07-1
Library of Congress Catalog Card Number: 00-104413

Printed in the United States of America

Most of the names in this book are real, but a few have been changed to protect privacy.

Cover Photo: © Mike Rastelli
Pee Wee Mercer riding Fire
Immokalee, FL., 1995

Dedicated
To

My mother and father, who helped me along the way; to Tracy, who helped me so much in the beginning; to all the old gang at Frontier Town in Maryland; and to all the rodeo cowboys I participated with.

Table
of
Contents

Illustrations

Prelude

Brighton, FL., Southeastern Circuit Finals, November 11, 1995. Pee Wee rides his last bull, V8. He broke his neck on this ride and the judges only gave him a 74. Photo: Mike Rastelli

My fiancée, Tracy, met me at Brighton, Florida to watch me participate in the Southeastern Circuit Finals rodeo. Only the top twelve bullriders in the Circuit go to the finals, and I was one of them. At the finals you ride three bulls.

Tracy was late getting there. She'd just flown back from Kansas City where she attended the National Future Farmers of America Convention. By the time she reached the arena I'd just been thrown from my first bull. I'd been on this bull twice before successfully, but this time he got the best of me. Nothing is certain in bullriding.

I was done for the day, so Tracy and I went back to the motel, which was 30 miles east in Okeechobee. Brighton is a Seminole Indian Reservation in the middle of nowhere, so most of the riders had to commute each day.

When we reached the motel we took showers and

went to bed. It had been a tiring day. We had a double bedroom suite on the second floor. Tracy slept in one room and I slept in the other.

The next morning, November 11, 1995 dawned just like any other day in Central Florida. The sky was a mixture of red-gray, and there was just a bare hint of fall in the air. There was nothing unusual about it.

Tracy went to McDonald's across the street for take-out breakfasts, and when she returned, we ate in the room. Then I got a call from Greg McManus, my traveling partner. He asked me to come downstairs and look at the new rigging-bags that were to be given away to the bullriders. I went down and picked out the one I wanted, then I went back to the room to get ready for the rodeo. It was scheduled to begin at 3 o'clock.

Tracy and I arrived at the arena about 2 o'clock, and I went immediately to see which bull I had drawn. When I saw my assigned bull I was surprised. It was V8, a 1600 pound juggernaut with a mixture of mischief and hostility in his eyes. I had been on this bull before and he had thrown me. I said to myself, "Not this time, old fellow."

The rodeo was delayed 2 hours because of a car wreck down the road, so I went to the concession stand to get two hotdogs. I didn't know it, but that would be the last thing I'd ever eat.

Bullriding is always the last event, so we had to wait longer than everyone else. Finally it was our turn. They bucked six bulls before they came to me. I got down on my bull, pulled my rope up tight, took my wrap, and then nodded my head. I had no idea that a doomsday clock was ticking, that in just a few seconds my life as I had known it would be changed forever.

When the gate opened, V8 stumbled but immediately got back to his feet. He started spinning to the left. I rode him through that, but when the whistle blew he jumped to the right, which hung me to the left. I am a right-hand bullrider, and you never want to come off the bull on the opposite side of the hand. When this happens, your hand will bind in the rope and you will be hung-up to the side of the bull.

I'd been hung-up before, lots of times, but this time was different. My right leg had gotten over my riding arm, and this pointed my head straight down. I was trying to get to the tail of the rope and release the bind. When I released it I landed on my head, and my head bent under my body. I was lying there unable to move. My friend, Greg McManus, was the first one to reach me. I said to him, "I think my neck is broken. I'm paralyzed."

We were so far from anywhere I had to be taken to the hospital by helicopter. During the flight the paramedics kept saying, "He's not going to make it."

I really don't know what I was thinking about during that flight. It could have been Tracy, or my parents, or my early childhood, or the first time I rode a horse or jumped on a bull. It's all kind of hazy. But I do know I could not move my body. It was as if I were encased in a solid block of ice.

As soon as we reached the hospital they did an MRI, and shortly after that a doctor came into the emergency room and said to me, "Your neck is broken, your spinal cord is severed. You will never walk again." He had sorrow in his eyes.

I said to him, "I'm not surprised," and that was it.

For the next three days the doctors kept telling my family I was going to die. I didn't, and I'm still here.

Chapter 1

Mercers

Glen "Pee Wee" Mercer in 1972, wearing his daddy's hat and readying to be a cowboy.

I have been a cowboy for as long as I can remember, probably from the day when I could first stand and walk alone. My daddy worked cattle for a living, doing what is known as "day work." That means he worked for different people. Believe me, the term day work doesn't mean you work just during the day. Many times, we worked long after dark. So I have been around cattle and horses all of my life.

Many tourists don't think of Florida as being a cattle state, but it was the original cattle state. There are still today something like two million head of cattle roaming the ranges, and many of those ranges stretch as far as the eye can see, and further.

I was born April 14, 1970 in Ocala, but I grew up in rural Levy County, outside Williston. My birth name is Glen Mercer, but I have always been known as Pee Wee. I weighed just a tad over four pounds when born. My mom could put my head in her hand, and my feet would just reach to the bend of her elbow. When my brother, who is 11 years older than me, would play with me, Mama would say, "Not so rough. He's just a little Pee Wee." And that name stuck like glue.

There were people who didn't know my real name is Glen until the rodeo accident happened to me. The Haddocks, who have known me all of my life, went to a high school rodeo where Bobby Haddock was a judge. His wife Sandy was watching for me to come out, but they announced me as Glen Mercer. After I rode, Sandy asked Bobby, "Who was that? He has the same last name as Pee Wee."

Bobby said, amused, "That WAS Pee Wee."

My Mercer family roots go back in Florida to the early part of the 19th Century, but the family can be traced back a long way. One of my ancestors, Christopher Mercer, died in 1671 in Barbados, West Indies. His son, Thomas, born in Barbados in 1648, settled in Norfolk County, Virginia in August 1669. From there, family members eventually drifted down into North Carolina, Georgia, and then into Florida.

One ancestor, Jesse Mercer, died in Butts County, Georgia in 1841. Although said to be moderately wealthy, his funeral was very simple. He was carried to the cemetery in a wagon with the mourners walking behind. There were no flowers, and the total cost of the funeral was said to be two dollars and fifty cents.

Many of the Mercers were Baptist ministers, both in Georgia, Mississippi, and Florida. Two of them, Herman and Joshua, both served as pastor of the Campbellton Baptist Church in Jackson County, Florida. This church was organized in 1825 and is the oldest Baptist Church in Florida. Joshua was also elected county commissioner of Jackson County in 1849, 4 years after Florida became a state. Other Mercers settled in Orange Hill, Florida in the early 1840s.

The Georgia Mercers started a school, Mercer Academy, in 1833, and this later became Mercer University.

My dad, Howard Mercer, was born in 1933 in Wausau, Florida, which back then was a one-horse town between Chipley and Panama City. My mom, who was Helen Lewis, was born in 1935 in Alabama.

Along the way there have been fairly well-to-do Mercers and dirt-poor Mercers – including preachers and educators and elected officials and businessmen and farmers and cattle drovers – but I feel certain that I am the only Mercer to ever become interested in bullriding.

Pee Wee Mercer & Big Boy, 1974

Chapter 2

**Memories
of
Dogs**

Pee Wee & Eat More Beef, who was
"great at getting cattle out of a
swamp or someplace."

Daddy had a lot of great cow dogs over the years,
and I still have memories of all of them. There was Tiger,
Sam, Queeny, Lady, Ike, Duke, B.J., Lepe, Pocket, Ruff, Tip,
Blackie, Lucky, Eat More Beef, and Teddy. All of them were
outstanding, and they all had something in common.

Some of them were head dogs, which means they got
ahead of the cattle and directed them where they needed
to go. Some were catch dogs, meaning if a cow broke out
of the herd they'd go after her and, let's say, teach her a
lesson. Or if a bull or cow holed up in a thicket or in a
pond, they'd make them move.

But like I said, they all had something in common:
they believed that the horses belonged to them, the horse
trailer belonged to them, and the barn was their property.
What that means is, if those dogs didn't know you, you'd
better not go anywhere near any of those things. If you
did, you were in deep trouble. You could rob our house
and take everything in it, and not a peep would come from

the dogs; but you'd better not go near the horses, the horse trailer, or the barn. All hell would break loose.

My first recollection is of Tiger and Sam. They were great cowdogs, but they would let me play with them, which some cowdogs aren't prone to do. When I was very young, I would ride on their backs around the yard, the same as riding a pony. I played with them so much I probably had more fleas than they did.

Tiger must have been a bulldog/bird-dog mix. He was very muscular, like a bulldog, and he was white with little red specs, like a bird-dog. There's a funny story about Tiger and a man named Jerry who once worked for my daddy. A cow had gone into a pond in Locklusa, a place known for gators. Tiger was swimming out to the cow, and at the same time, a gator was swimming toward Tiger. Jerry rode his horse out to Tiger, picked him up out of the water, and carried him up the bank to safety. Tiger should have been thankful, because Jerry saved his life. But Tiger must have been mad about Jerry interrupting him while doing his job – he bit the stew out of Jerry.

On the other hand, one day Daddy and another guy were holding up a bunch of cattle while two other guys were trying to get a cow out of a pond. Daddy said, "Tiger, go help those boys." Off he went, and he got the cow out.

Another thing all those dogs had in common: they listened to Daddy.

Sam was a big hairy dog, colored black and brown. He was mostly Rottweiler, but he was mixed with something else. We never were sure about the mix, because Sam was given to Daddy.

One day Daddy and his helpers were driving a bunch of cattle to the pen when one cow broke out and went into the woods. Daddy sent Sam to get her. They waited and waited, but there was no sign of the cow or Sam, so they drove the rest of the cattle to the pen. About thirty minutes later, here comes Sam and that cow. He was behind her, and every time she'd stop, Sam would nip her to keep her going. He brought that cow all the way to the pen by himself.

Then there was Queeny. She was bred out of two leopard dogs, but she came out red and white. Leopard dogs are supposed to be black and blue and gray spotted. The main thing I remember about Queeny is something that happened between her and Mama. One day, Mama went out to get something out of Daddy's truck. Queeny must have been asleep and didn't see her, but when Mama turned around to go back to the house, there stood Queeny. She wouldn't let Mama go back to the house, and she wouldn't let her go back to the truck. Mama must have stood out there screaming for Daddy for a half-hour before he finally wondered where she was. He couldn't hear her because of the TV. He finally went to see what was wrong, and when he saw what was happening, he just started laughing. Mama screamed at him like you wouldn't believe, and he called off the dog. Daddy sold a lot of puppies out of Queeny, and they were all good cowdogs.

B.J. was a cur dog, yellow with white feet and a white nose. Some curs have black noses, and those are the best, but there are exceptions. The most peculiar thing about B.J. was that nobody could touch him. I mean nobody. He would load-up in the trailer, work cattle, listen well and carry out instructions, but you just couldn't touch him. When we had to give him his vaccination, we'd fool him. We'd load a horse on the trailer and he'd think we were going to work, then we'd put a rope around his neck and pull him into a corner. He would eat your hand off if you weren't careful. When we roped B.J. he wasn't hurt, just scared.

Lady, Duke, Pocket, Tip and Ruff were all curs, and they were good head dogs. If a herd broke they would run as far as they had to to reach the front and stop them.

Blackie and Eat More Beef were, I guess, what you'd call mutts. They were so mixed that you really couldn't see one breed stand out in them. One thing for sure, they had bulldog in them, because they were strictly catch dogs. If a cow went into a thicket they'd make her come out, and when she did, the cow would usually be bleeding from the nose and ears. They'd eat her head off if she didn't move. That may sound cruel, but sometimes that is the only way to get bad cows to pay attention and stay with the herd.

Lucky was a mutt too, and a catch dog, but the way he got his name is interesting as well as unusual. One day Daddy and a friend, Emery Mills, were looking for some cattle that had gotten out and strayed onto another man's property. The foreman of the place rode up to them in his truck and stopped. While they were talking, they saw a dog walking across the field. Now, the last thing you want is a stray dog around, especially during calving season, so the foreman took out his hunting rifle, got the dog in his sights, and fired. The bullet hit under the dog's feet. The foreman fired again, and missed again, then the dog started running directly towards them. The foreman fired again, and again he missed. The dog ran straight to Daddy, as if he knew him, and sat down beside him, pushing close.

The foreman said, "I don't understand this. I sighted this gun yesterday. It was dead on."

From that day on, this stray was our dog, and we named him Lucky. It just so happened he became a good cowdog.

Teddy was a sheep dog, but he was a good cowdog. The funniest thing I remember about Teddy is that after a day of working cattle he'd fall asleep on the back of the truck. Daddy had a flat-bed truck, and when he turned off the road coming home, Teddy would roll off, then he'd have to walk about 2 miles home. Sometimes Daddy would stop and let him back on, but sometimes Daddy would forget that Teddy always did that, and Teddy would have to walk.

Seems Teddy would learn better, but he never did.

Chapter 3

Memories
of
Horses

As they parade in front of me in my memory, their names come back easily: Big Boy, Pepper, Buck, Little Red, Billy, Bill, and Black. They were all outstanding horses, each with a distinct personality.

Big Boy was a cracker horse, a bay with a white blaze. He was a good cow horse, but the main thing I remember about him is that he taught me and my brother to ride. Daddy would come home at the end of the day, and as tired as Big Boy would be, he would let us hang all over him. I'd grab the bridle reins, and Big Boy would lift his head up and let me swing back and forth. I would even crawl between his legs. Big Boy would let me do anything. At this time I was still in diapers, but Daddy would set me up on Big Boy and lead him around. Yes, thanks to Big Boy, I could ride a horse before I could walk. Big Boy died on our place when he was about 30 years old.

Pepper was a quarter horse, red with four stockings and a white blaze. In my daddy's opinion, Pepper was the best horse he ever owned. He said that nobody but him could rope off of Pepper. Mama loved riding him, but I didn't like him because the one time I did ride him he threw me off – but I was only 4 years old. Pepper was retired to a beautiful place that belongs to some friends of ours. He died at the age of thirty-three, back in 1995.

Little Red was also a quarter horse, a bay, and he was my horse – well, kinda. Daddy worked cattle with him, but I still called him mine. The best story I like to tell about Little Red is a time when a friend borrowed him to hunt deer off of him. He said he just wanted him for a week, but after three weeks he still didn't return him. So one day my cousin, Terry, was visiting, and we were going to the store. My friend's house was between our house and the store, about a mile from us. I asked Terry to drop me off there. I was going to get my horse back. I went to the barn where Little Red was housed, but I couldn't find a bridle; so I just jumped on him without one, and away we went – home! Most horses would run off with you without a bridle, but Little Red wouldn't hurt me for anything. Little Red got a bowed tendon in his left front leg and had to be put down.

Buck is a buckskin. That's why we call him Buck, although my brother might say it's for another reason. My brother broke Buck, and he said he'd never had a horse buck so hard with him in all his life. But he must have gotten all of that out of him, because I've never seen him buck. In my opinion, that's the best horse Daddy ever owned. He was so fast, and you could rope just about anything off of him. Example: Daddy has roped buffalo, camels, llamas and zebras off of Buck. We once worked for an exotic animal farm, and they had everything – literally – from A to Z. Buck is still alive and well, and he is here at our place.

Billy was a quarter horse, a bay. She was very fast too, but she had a little flaw: she kept throwing my daddy off. She put him in the hospital twice. One of the best stories about her happened one day when my mama was riding her in our arena. Daddy was riding another horse at the same time. All of a sudden Billy threw mama off and ran straight to Daddy. Mama screamed, "I'll never get on you again!"

We ended up selling Billy to a rodeo company. She was to be used as a bucking horse, and she did very well. Hardly anyone ever rode her successfully, and when they did, they won first place. This brings me to the best story about her. We went to a rodeo in Callahan, and the local people were having what's known as a "cracker day." As part of that, they were having horse races. There was no entry fee, and you'd win money if you came in first. I knew Billy was very fast, so I asked a stock contractor, who was a friend, if I could borrow Billy and one of his saddles. After he stopped laughing, he said fine. He thought Billy would throw me off, and that would be the end of that. Everyone would get a good laugh. Well, Billy not only did not throw me off, we won the race. That very night, Billy stopped bucking. The stock contractor's son started riding her. He loved her, and she became his horse. As far as I know, he still has her.

Bill was Billy's son and also the son of a great horse named Mr. Perfection. Bill was black like his daddy, and they were both quarter horses. Bill was really, really fast, but he was hard to control. He was so big and powerful. I remember once when I was riding Bill and we went to head off a big bull – I mean a big bull, weighing about 2,100 pounds. We were running beside the bull when all of a sudden Bill darted into him and knocked him down, then Bill and I ran over him. I guess Bill got tired of running beside the bull and decided to put an end to it. Bill eventually died from a twisted gut – that's when horses get kind of a stomach ache. They can't throw up like some animals do in a similar situation, so they roll on their backs from side to side, sometimes twisting their gut. If you catch it early enough you can oil their stomachs. This will make their bowels move, and they won't hurt anymore, but we didn't catch it early enough with Bill.

Black was the best horse I've ever owned, but Black wasn't really black – he was black and brown. If there's one thing I want to do in this book, it's to make you understand the bond between myself and Black. We were friends, not just a horse and his rider.

One day a friend of ours asked Daddy if he would take this horse off his hands and try to ride him. Daddy said yes, but he told the man he'd have to pay the feed bill. The man agreed, and Daddy brought this horse home.

Black was a pitiful sight. He was a cross between a cracker and a quarter horse. His legs were so skinny they'd probably break if you got in rough terrain. His body was very skinny too, and if he'd ever been fed, you couldn't tell it by looking at him. We took care of him and fed him until he could at least carry someone on his back.

I wasn't the one who first started riding Black – it was Jimmy, a man who worked for Daddy. Jimmy had one problem with riding horses: he was blind in his right eye. At that time I had another horse, one I haven't mentioned because he wasn't much to talk about. Anyway, one day Daddy and me were going to pen some cattle. I didn't have a horse to ride (I'd sold my horse), so Daddy told me to ride Black. When we started penning the cattle, Black wouldn't turn fast enough. Jimmy hadn't taught him to do that because Jimmy, being blind in one eye, couldn't stay on if he turned fast. Black and I weren't much help but we got the cattle to the pen, thanks mostly to the cowdogs.

When we got home later that day, I started training Black, and I didn't stop for three months. I guess we really bonded, because after that, nobody else could ride him – he'd throw them off. Don't get me wrong – he's thrown me off more times than I'd like to admit. But Black had so much personality we understood each other – kinda.

I decided I wanted to make a calf roping horse out of Black. There were a few people who said I'd never make anything out of him, but Daddy bought me six calves, and we started. I had my own arena right here at the house.

One day, after Black and I had worked together for two months, one of those doubters came out to our house. I was in the arena roping. The man said to me, "Are you still messing with that no good horse?"

I didn't say anything. I backed Black into the box, dropped the reins on his neck and then nodded for my calf. When the calf came out, Black was right on him. Black tracked him all the way to the other end, then I roped the calf. Black stopped just like he was supposed to, and he worked the rope for me just like he was supposed to. When we were done, I rode back up to the man and said, "What do you think now about this no good horse?"

He just looked at me with amazement, then he shook his head and walked off.

I could rope anything off of Black – bulls, cows, steers, it didn't matter. He was a great horse.

A funny story I like to tell about Black: he was the kind of horse that if you didn't ride him every day, he'd try to buck you off, even me. I'd just come back from Maryland, and Black hadn't been ridden by anybody in about three weeks, so I knew he was going to buck with me. I was ready for him, I thought. We worked together all week and he never tried anything, so by Friday I relaxed. We were riding back to the pen that morning. My butt was sore, so I slid out of the saddle and back onto his butt. I'd done that a thousand times before, but this time he looked back at me, started bucking, and threw me off. Then he just stood there looking at me, kinda grinning, and I swear he was saying, "Got ya!"

As I said, our relationship was more than a horse and his rider. I loved Black, and I'm sure he loved me too. I was nineteen when he died, and I cried like a baby. He died of a twisted gut, like Bill. We buried him right here on our place, next to the barn.

I've never owned another horse since Black. I've ridden hundreds of them, but that's all. No other horse could replace Black, not in my heart or my memory. I miss him so much, and always will.

Pee Wee practices on a Brahma Bull in a private arena at a Lake City, FL. bull riding school.

Chapter 4

**My
Start
in
Rodeo**

Gainesville, FL., 1985. Pee Wee, after a winning 72 point ride on Rodeo Red, gets hung up trying to dismount. His right boot gone and his glove twisted in the rope he had to jump over the bull to free his hand. He gave his First Prize buckle to a hospitalized friend. Photo: Mike Rastelli

Although I had been "knee deep" in cattle and horses since I was a toddler, my fascination with rodeo and bullriding didn't start until about 1978. Our next door neighbors, the Whilldens, who lived about a quarter-mile from us, had a son, Greg, who was like a big brother to me. He took me almost everywhere he went. My own big brother wasn't around very much, so Greg was it.

I loved Greg and wanted to be just like him. Greg rode bulls in high school rodeos. I wanted to do that too, but I was too young. Greg was such an influence on me and I sometimes did foolish things. When I was in the 3rd grade, Greg came to pick me up after school. His girlfriend worked there, so he lingered awhile to spend time with her. I stayed right with them. When this guy who was in the 8th grade came walking past, Greg said, "I'll bet you can't whip him."

That guy was three times my size, but I beat the heck out of him just because Greg said that. To say the least, I wanted Greg's approval of everything I did. I wanted him to be proud of me. Because Greg rode bulls, I started out riding calves, and everyone thought it was funny.

One day Greg went with my daddy to help work some cattle. There was a bad bull in the pen, and they couldn't get in there with him. Daddy sent the dogs in. One of our best cowdogs was coming into the pen when the bull saw him, ran over to him, and hooked the dog's guts out. When Greg saw this he got sick and swore he'd never ride bulls again, but I didn't change my mind.

When I was old enough, which was in 1983 when I was thirteen, I got a chance to enter a junior rodeo. There had never been a junior rodeo before so my friend, Will Strickland, and I went. We entered the bareback bronco riding and the bullriding. We borrowed his cousin's old rodeo equipment. It was pretty ragged, but it was all we had. We shared the bareback rigging, the bull rope, and the gloves.

Will was up first, and he got thrown off. Then it was my turn. I got down on the horse, put my hand in the rigging, and nodded my head. When the gates opened, I jerked my feet back, then the back of my head hit the ground. I was kinda dazed and confused. I lifted my arm, and there was the rigging still in my hand. The lasso had broken.

They gave me a re-ride, and I won second. Then it was time for the bullriding. I was very nervous. I had never been on a bull this big. He weighed about eleven hundred pounds, and I found out later that this was small. I pulled my rope, got a good seat, and nodded my head. That's all I remember.

When you first start riding, the adrenaline is so great that you black out. You are still conscious, but you can't remember anything about the ride. This happens on about your first thirty or thirty-five bulls. It's not too dangerous because your mind and your body will react.

Anyway, we had only five junior rodeos that year, including the State Finals in Lakeland. Will and I went into a McDonald's in Lakeland, and after eating, we came back outside. We were sitting on the fender of the horse trailer, imitating the older rodeo riders by taking a dip of Copenhagen as we thought we should do, when a kid came in and parked his car on a slight incline in front of our truck. After he got out and went inside, his car started backing out by itself. He had failed to put it in park. That car backed right into our trailer, at the spot we were sitting. It barely missed us. It scared the heck out of us, even worse than riding a bull. Anyway, as it had turned out, I had stopped riding bulls and stuck to horses. I won the bareback championship. The next year I would be old enough to go into high school rodeo.

The year was 1985 and I was in my first year at Williston High School. I was eligible to compete in high school rodeo. I thought I was a good bareback rider, but things change. My daddy talked me into riding bulls too. I thought it was a mistake, but as I said, things change.

At the first rodeo, I rode my horse but was thrown off of my bull. At the second rodeo, I won the bareback riding and was again thrown off of my bull. By this time I'd started riding saddle broncos too. I told my daddy that if I didn't ride my bull at the third rodeo I was going to quit doing that. He agreed.

At the next rodeo I was thrown off my bareback horse and my saddle bronco, but I rode my bull and won second place. As the year wore on I got better and better at bullriding, and I ended up winning the State Championship in bullriding and the average at the State Finals. This made me eligible to enter the High School National Finals in Rapid City, South Dakota.

Earlier that year a good friend of mine, Roland Cortes, shattered his lower left leg when he was thrown from his bull at a rodeo in Gainesville. He was the rider just before my turn, and when I saw him hit the ground, I was very concerned about him. I ran out into the arena to check on him.

Just as I reached Roland a man named Homer Cannon, who had known me all of my life, rushed up and shouted, "Get back behind those chutes! You've still got a bull to ride!"

Although I was shaky, I rode my bull and won the bullriding, then I had my mom and dad take me immediately to the hospital where Roland was.

We got there just before they took him into surgery. Roland had never won a buckle, so I handed him my new buckle and said, "This is for you."

He took that buckle with him into surgery, and, I think, he still wears it to this very day.

I had to quit riding saddle broncos because of a little accident. At a rodeo in Starke I rode my saddle bronco horse successfully but my foot got hung in the stirrup, causing me to hit the ground. The horse stepped on the back of my head, driving my face into the dirt and knocking me out.

When they got to me I was choking on the dirt in my mouth. Mr. Emery lifted my head and started digging the dirt out so I could breathe. As they rushed me away to the hospital, Mama and Daddy were scared to death. It turned out later to be just a bump on the head.

When Mama reached the hospital I was awake. She looked straight at me, wagged her finger and said, "You can sell that saddle, or burn it, but you'll never ride it again!"

I didn't.

It was then time to head out for the Finals in Rapid City. Thirty-three states and two Canadian provinces sent their best to this event. Being among this group was heady stuff for a 15-year-old kid from rural Levy County. The top four in each event reach the finals.

Mama and Daddy took me there in our '83 Chevy van, and my friend Roland went with us. There was a couch and a make-shift bed in the van, and to be honest with you, I slept most of the way – I missed a lot of beautiful scenery. It was just over a three-day trip.

When we reached Rapid City we intended to stay in a motel, but that plan changed. My mama's sister from California had driven there just for the rodeo, and she had a nice RV. She was at a campground, so we went there and also got a space for our van. It turned out to be much more fun than a motel.

When it came time for me to ride my first bull, there was a wind storm. So much sand was flying around I could hardly see. I put a raincoat over my head so I could open my eyes enough to set my rope. When they opened the gate, I just fell off. By the time of my second bull the weather was better, but he threw me off too.

Although I didn't win, we all had a lot of fun. We stayed for all seven days of the rodeo and attended two events each day, at 9 a.m. and again at 7 p.m. Roland and I met a lot of kids who also had never been so far from home, and we had a ball with them.

Going home, would you believe that I slept most of the way again.

Chapter 5

An Unusual Accident

Homestead, FL., 1985. Florida High School Rodeo Association (FHSRA) event. Pee Wee riding Sunshine for his first win in a high school rodeo. Photo: Mike Rastelli

An unusual thing happened to me after I got back from the finals. I went with Daddy one morning to work some cattle. One cow wouldn't go in the pen. She was blind, so I decided to rope her.

It was back when I had Black. When we went out to rope the cow she heard us coming and took off running, so we broke in behind her.

The dew was still on the ground, and it was slippery. Just as I stood up in the saddle to throw my rope, the cow slipped down. Black fell over her, and we both went down. When we fell I broke my left leg but did not know it.

When the cow got up, she was very scared and mad. Black also got up. He was a little shaken but not injured. Like I said, the cow was blind and also mad. The only way she could catch me was if I made any noise.

I didn't know my leg was broken until I tried to stand

up, and then it hit me. I let out a yell. The cow was about 15 feet away. She heard me and started toward me, and there wasn't anything I could do.

The cow was about half way to me when, out of nowhere, our good cowdog, Doc, came from behind me and attacked the cow. I had named him Doc because he was a bulldog, but his tail was long, not docked. He kept the cow away from me and held her there for someone else to rope. The guys helping us were not that good with a rope.

My leg was broken in nine places. I used crutches for three weeks and was supposed to stay on them for six weeks, but I got tired of trying to get around school with them, and discarded them before I was supposed to. This placed all the burden of walking on the cast alone.

When I went back to the doctor, he said to me, "What in the hell have you done to this cast?"

I said, "I've just been walking on it, and lifting weights. You know, not too much."

He gave me a queer look, and then he said, "Well, it must be healed then. We'll just take it off."

Remember, I was only fifteen. I healed fast then. But don't all kids?

Chapter 6

**New
Belt
for
My
New
Buckle**

Ocala, FL., 1986. 16-year-old Pee Wee, in his first professional rodeo, ties for First Place scoring 79 points riding Spider. Photo: Mike Rastelli

The next year, 1986, I was ineligible to compete in high school rodeo because my grades were too bad. Although high school rodeo is not affiliated with one particular high school, you have to maintain a certain grade point average in order to compete. So I went to some "open rodeos." They pay money if you win. High school doesn't. I also entered my first professional rodeo. It was in Ocala, and it was the annual rodeo. I entered as a local, but you can't do that anymore.

After Daddy told me I was entered, I was really excited, but when we got there, the butterflies started. I was more nervous than excited. I went to see which bull I'd drawn. He was number two, and his name was Spider. Now, I'm not afraid of many things, but I've got a fear of spiders that's unbelievable.

That fear might have helped me. When Spider came into the chute he was very small, but his horns were pretty long. He started hooking at everything. I became even more nervous.

It was my turn now. Remember, I'm only sixteen. I got down on the bull, and someone pulled my rope for me. I nodded my head, and they opened the gate.

Spider took three jumps out, then he spun to the right. I ride bulls better if they turn back into my riding hand. Most bullriders do. Anyway, when he started spinning I couldn't help myself – I started spurring him with my outside foot. You get more points if you do that. When the whistle blew, I jumped off. I was so happy. I had ridden a professional bucking bull! Then they called out my score – 79 points! I was winning the bullriding at a P.R.C.A. rodeo.

P.R.C.A. stands for Professional Rodeo Cowboys Association. I ended up tieing for first, but that didn't really matter. I got the champion buckle! It said, "Ocala Shriner Rodeo Champion Bullrider 1986." And I won over six hundred dollars! That's a lot of money to a 16-year-old. I'd won money before, but not that much at once.

The first thing I bought, of course, was a new belt for my buckle. The belt was gray with silver conchos. It's important to know about the belt, for towards the end of this book it will still be there.

In 1987 my grades were up a lot, so I went back to high school rodeo. I did continue riding in those open rodeos, and that's how I made enough money to go to my junior prom – which was a disaster, not for me so much, but for my date. We went in her car. The prom was so boring that I left her there to go to another party alone. The worst part is, I took her car. It wasn't grand-theft auto. Her mom had given me permission to drive. But never-the-less, my date had to find a ride home. I took the car straight to her house and had some friends pick me up there, but I had left my date stranded temporarily. This did not endear me to anyone.

Chapter 7

On
to
Colorado

I didn't do too well that year in high school rodeo, but I finished third in the state. This qualified me to go to the National Finals again, and this time they were to be held in Pueblo, Colorado.

Colorado is the most beautiful state I've ever seen, but before I went there, my destination was Maryland. I had a friend who got me a job at Frontier Town in Ocean City. Frontier Town is a western theme park. They put on shows like gunfights, Can-Can shows, demonstrations of rodeos, trail rides, and real Indian dancing. The Finals were at the end of July, so I went to Frontier Town in June. I was to return there for a time after the Finals.

When I left Frontier Town, I rode a bus to Colorado. Take my advice and never ride a bus across six states unless you have to. This was without a doubt the worst experience of my life. The bus itself wasn't too bad, it was the things that happened along the way.

During a 3-hour layover in St. Louis, I was sitting watching television in one of those TV chairs. You know, the ones you put a quarter in. Anyway, a shady looking man sat down next to me and asked me if I wanted to buy a woman for a while. I got up immediately and moved away from him.

While walking to the restroom I noticed this girl who was scared to death. A tall raunchy man with no teeth had her cornered, and was talking to her. Her face had the terror of a fox caught in a steel trap. On my way back from the restroom, I did something that surprised even me. As I passed by where she was sitting, I said, "Amy, is that you?"

She didn't hesitate. She jumped up immediately, hugged me and said, "David! It's so good to see you! How've you been?"

We didn't know each other from Adam's Aunt, but it didn't matter. That man had her so scared she just hugged me again. Then we left together. Her name was Rachel, and she was going to Golden, so we were on the same bus for some time.

This incident happened in a bus station just past the Colorado border. I started to get on the bus my ticket indicated was the right one. The bus driver looked at my ticket and said, "If you get on this other bus, you'll get there a day earlier."

I was so tired of buses that I just said thanks and ran for the other bus. That was a mistake. My mom and dad had driven out from Florida before me, and they expected to pick me up at the bus station the next day. When we arrived in Pueblo, there was no one there to meet me. I felt a touch of panic. I was stranded alone in an unfamiliar place, with nowhere to go, and no one to help me.

I finally walked down the street to a cab station and asked if someone would take me to the fairgrounds where the rodeo was being held. The cab driver who volunteered was a large man, very hairy everywhere except on his head.

He wasn't someone you'd want to meet in a dark alley. To him, I probably looked like some young country hick who was ripe for plucking.

As it turned out, he was a very nice person. He drove me around the fairgrounds three times, and the grounds were huge. There was only one gate open to the inside, so I asked him to let me out there. I said, "How much do I owe you?"

"Four dollars," he said.

I had only three dollars and some change in my pocket. There was over three hundred dollars hidden away in my boot, but I didn't want to bring that out. I was still nervous about this man.

Then he said, "Three dollars is fine."

I felt sorry then for mistrusting him so much. I shook his hand, thanked him, and got out of the cab.

The only open gate was where they were unloading the stock. I had a heavy suitcase in one hand, and my rigging bag over my shoulder. I walked about a half-mile, looking constantly. I knew my mom and dad were somewhere on the fairgrounds, but where?

I sat down on a bench to rest. I must have looked pretty forlorn, because the first car that came along pulled in and stopped. A man and a woman were inside. The man leaned out the window and asked if I needed help.

I said, "I'm trying to find the Florida people. Do you know where they're staying?"

The man said, "I know where Mr. Kruger is."

Mr. Kruger was the National Director from Florida, and also a very nice man. I asked if they would take me to him, and the man said sure, get in. As it turned out, they were Mr. and Mrs. Custer from Arizona and their son, Cody

Custer, was a World Champion bullrider.

On the way to find Mr. Kruger, I saw my mom's van. I said, "There's my mom and dad. Please let me out here."

When we pulled in and stopped, I got out immediately and went to the trunk to get my things. Mom walked out to the car and the woman said to her, "We've got something that belongs to you."

Mom hadn't seen me yet, so she said, "I don't think so."

Then she saw me. We ran to each other and hugged, then we thanked both of them, hoping we would see them again.

The next thing I said to mom was, "I'm flying back when this is over. I'm not riding another bus."

We all had a great time together in Colorado. The Finals were fun, but again I didn't win. After it ended, I flew back to Maryland, to Frontier Town.

There's one thing I should mention about that flight – I'm afraid of heights. When I got ready to board that airplane it was worse than getting on the back of any bull I've ever known. I was scared stiff. It was a 30-seater. Two friends were on the same airplane, and Mama had asked them to try to keep me calm. They talked to me constantly, telling me there's nothing to be afraid of.

They were still talking after the airplane took off, but I didn't hear a word. I was looking out the window, and I'd never seen anything like this.

After we got to Denver we went our separate ways, then I got on one of those really big airplanes. It flew so high there was nothing to see. We landed in Baltimore, then I got on a very small plane, so small it was called a "puddle jumper," to continue on to Ocean City. This plane had two propellers on its wings, and behind the props were two big compartments, which I thought contained the engines. When they started loading those compartments with luggage, I almost passed out.

When I got off that airplane in Ocean City, I didn't know if I would kiss the ground or throw up, but I did start thinking more kindly about buses.

To top it off, they lost my luggage. I finally got it back three days later.

Deland, FL., 1987. Pee Wee riding Black Magic in an FHSRA bull riding competition. Photo: Mike Rastelli

Chapter 8

Frontier Town

Frontier Town, as I said before, is a western theme park and a really great "family park." Shows are performed in front of live audiences, so there are no second takes. You either get it right the first time, or you screw up. At that point in my life I was very shy around people, but I had to get over that fast.

No one played the same part all of the time. You did what you were assigned to do. Sometimes you played the outlaw, and outlaws always die. Sometimes you played the good guy, and good guys never get shot. Sometimes you played the drunk in the Can-Can show, and this is known as comic relief.

There were several bunkhouses inside the park for employees who wanted to stay there – mostly "out-of-towners," like me. Most of the employees did not stay in the park. There was a small bunkhouse over the Leather Shop, one over the Barber Shop, and a larger one over the General Store. I was assigned to the one over the

Leather Shop.

My first day at work I was assigned to play the barber in the Barber Shop, which meant that I shaved kids with a straight razor with a fake blade. They also asked me to move around and see all of the shows, because the next day I would play different roles and they wanted me to be familiar with all of them.

The only area I was not nervous about was the rodeo section. I could ride a horse with the best of them, and the other guys who worked there couldn't. Most of them were from Maryland and Pennsylvania, and you don't find many cowboys up that way.

About 3 o'clock the streets were quiet, and I was sitting outside the Barber Shop resting. Across the street was Aunt Mary's Candy Store. A girl came out of the store, then she noticed me and waved to me. I'm not good-looking at all, and I wondered why she was waving at me. She came across the street and said, "I'm Jennifer. Who are you?"

I said, "I'm Pee Wee." And then I said, "That's just my nickname. My real name is Glen Mercer."

She said, "Are you from Florida? I heard someone is joining us from there."

She probably already knew, from my Southern accent, where I was from. I said, "Yeah. I'm from Florida."

She asked me what I was doing and I explained that I was playing the barber but was supposed to move around and see all the shows because tomorrow I would play different roles. She then told me that a Can-Can show was just about to start.

The Can-Can show was the hardest to learn because you played the drunk and there were lots of lines to learn and remember. As I took off running toward the Golden Nugget Saloon, I yelled back, "See ya' later."

My first meeting with Jennifer was a brief one, but after all these years, I can still remember what she was wearing: a blue and white checkered short-sleeved shirt that buttoned in the front, and faded blue jeans. She was very pretty, with brown curly hair and brown eyes. She looked like Molly Ringwald without the red hair and snow-white skin.

I met a lot of interesting people at Frontier Town. There was Eddie, who had lots of hair and dimples so deep you could almost see through his face when he smiled. He was from Salisbury, not far from Ocean City. Then there was Gino, who also had long hair and looked kinda scruffy. His home was also not far from Ocean City, but he and Eddie lived in the bunkhouse at the park. There was Tim, the park manager, from up-state New York. He was our boss, but he was cool. There were others, but I don't remember them as well.

All of the Can-Can dancers were from Pennsylvania. There was Lisa, Anne, Anna, and Sharon. Lisa and I were good friends, and that made her boyfriend, J.T., mad. I almost forgot to mention J.T. He was 6 feet tall and he was only 16 years old.

During the day we did our jobs as best we could. None of us were professional actors, but everyone seemed to enjoy the shows anyway. Maybe our occasional bumbling as amateurs made the performances more interesting.

After the park closed at night, we all got together. We ate and told tall tales. This included everyone except the Can-Can girls. Rather than staying in a bunkhouse at the park, they lived in a rented house in Ocean City and left each night as soon as the park closed. But they finally did come around, and they joined us occasionally.

The most memorable thing about those night-time parties was, during your performance the next day, you could slip into your lines something foolish someone had done or said the night before. The audience wouldn't catch it, but the person you were telling it on would. They would usually laugh and then mess up their own lines. One night during a party someone said, "You're as crazy as a run over coon." This guy, Todd, repeated it as, "Ya ya run over coon." We started saying that during the shows and someone would always crack up.

The real story of that summer, for me, was the chance to get on so many bulls and steers in the rodeo section. Getting on the steers helped me because they were small and this taught me to use my feet more. The bulls were powerful, and getting on them taught me to get over the front, to take the power away.

And Jennifer. Man, did I have a crush on Jennifer! First love – you know how it is. I was completely smitten. I think Jennifer taught me how to love, because up until then, I'd never felt that way about any girl.

Chapter 9

My
Senior
Year
1988

When I left Maryland in September I had missed two weeks of my senior year. Adjusting back to routine school days was tough after such an experience as Frontier Town, but I tried hard. I made up all of my work, and I made the honor roll that semester. All in all, my senior year was really great.

I had gone out for football in spring practice. I would have been a starter on defense and offense, but I couldn't do rodeo and play football too, so I chose rodeo. I was good at football, but I was better at rodeo. Besides, there isn't much future in football for someone who is 5'5" tall and weighs 135 pounds.

I didn't participate much in other school activities. Rodeo was my life, and my hopes and dreams were just to ride bulls. Everyone knew me as a bullrider. I was popular with my fellow students, but some of my black classmates thought that – because I rode bulls – I must have been crazy. Maybe I was.

I did hang out a lot with several good friends. One of them was Taco. His real name was Thomas Alvarez. He wanted a nickname so the guys at the high school rodeos started calling him Taco. He started riding bulls too, but he wasn't very good at it.

There was also Tammy. We hung out at her house a lot because her dad thought we were all cool. Later in the year another person became a good friend – Kelly Richmond. She was an exchange student from Australia, and I loved her Australian accent. She had never been to a rodeo so we took her with us to a couple of them, and she enjoyed them. Sometimes she was funny because she didn't know American culture very well and she would also get tripped up on words. I once played her a song called "Amarillo by Morning," and she thought the singer was saying "Armadillo Good Morning."

Another great thing about that year was when Daddy bought some bucking bulls for us to practice on. Every Sunday, when there were no rodeos, we would get together at my house and practice. This included Taco, Steve Snow, and Rusty Byrd. We would practice almost all day, then we would all get in Steve's truck and ride around listening to music, mostly George Strait.

I did well that year in high school rodeo. We had sixteen rodeos and I won seven of them. I placed no worse than 3rd in four of them and was thrown off in four. I was disqualified in four because I hit the bull with my free hand.

I might explain a few things about bullriding. First, the rules: Riding is to be done with one hand and the other hand cannot touch the bull nor the rider. Riding is done with a regulation bull rope with bells attached. No hooks or extra knots are allowed. Bullriding spur rowels must be locked. A rider must stay on for eight seconds. If any of the above is violated, the rider is disqualified.

What all of this means is that a regulation bull rope is a flat braided rope with a hand hold braided into the rope. One side is where your loop is, and that's where your bells are attached. The bells are there to pull the rope off after you've been thrown off, or get off. The other side is the tail. It goes through your loop and back to your hand. You have to adjust your loop to the size of the bull to make sure you have enough tail. You have to have enough tail because after you have pulled the rope as tight as you like, you need enough tail to wrap the rope behind your hand and back into your hand. Then you have to make sure you have enough left to be able to grab it and release the bind you created, to get off safely. Sound complicated? It's really not. It just takes practice.

The term "pulled my rope" means that the person standing on the side of the chute pulls the rope tight around the bull's body, then he hands the tail of the rope to me. I take it in my hand, pull it tighter if it needs this, then I wrap the rope (take my wrap) around my right hand. Stated the simplest way, "pulled my rope" means to tighten it around the bull's body and pass the tail of the rope on to me.

The free hand is also for a reason – it helps you keep your balance. The rowels are locked because they will grip the bull's hide instead of rolling. And, of course, you have to make the 8-second whistle without touching yourself or the bull with your free hand.

Bullriding is a combination of strength, balance, finesse, and ability. You have to have finesse because there is no way you are going to out-strength a bull. No way!

It was in October when I went to the first rodeo of my senior year. I drew a bull that hadn't been ridden much, but I stayed on him and won the bullriding. I was off to a good start.

When I got home from the rodeo I called Jennifer to tell her about my win. I also wanted to tell her something else. I was nervous because what I wanted to tell her was that I loved her.

Well, I beat around the bush for awhile, and then I said, "There's something I want to say, but I'm not sure how to say it."

Jennifer broke in and said, "I think I know what it is." Then she said, "I love you."

I was shocked, but I immediately said "I love you" back to her. I was relieved and excited at the same time. It felt as if all the blood drained from my body in less than a second, then it returned all at once.

Jennifer sent me lots of letters, but I didn't write back, except for a couple of times. I wasn't much into writing. I was more of the kind to make a phone call. But as it turned out later, she had a new boyfriend. As a matter of fact, he was at her house the night she told me she loved me. I guess those words come easier for some people.

When I reached the State Finals I was only ten points ahead of the guy in second place. I knew I had to ride very good. The guy in second place came out on his bull and scored 72 points, then the guy in third scored 73, making him only fifteen points behind me in the state standings. I had a lot of pressure, but I didn't let it get to me.

I got on my bull and had someone pull my rope, but the bull was bad in the chute, so I had to call for him standing over him, not sitting on his back. That's preferred. When they opened the gate I jumped at him and got a good seat. He bucked out two jumps and started spinning to the left, then I started spurring him with my right leg. Remember, you get more points for doing that. When the whistle blew and I jumped off, they announced my score as 76. I won that round but there were two more to go.

I won the next round too because everyone else got thrown off, so that meant I was already State Champion. In the third round I was the last one to ride. Everyone else had been thrown off so I had already won the average too. But I really wanted to ride this bull. He was the first bull I had ridden at the first rodeo of the year, and he hadn't been ridden since.

I got down on the bull and someone pulled my rope for me, but the bull was leaning on my right leg. We tried everything to get him off my leg, but I finally called for him like that. That's not good either. He came out ducking and diving left and right. Bulls are hard to ride when they

Pee Wee in the 1988 FHSRA Finals riding Beetle Bomb. Photo: Mike Rastelli

do that, but I rode him. When the whistle blew and I jumped off, the judges said I hit him with my free hand, so they disqualified me. That was totally untrue! I never touched that bull with my free hand. No matter, I was the average winner and the State Champion. That meant another trip to Pueblo.

I said that my senior year was a really great year, but one incident almost made it the worst. It happened on the first day of the Ocala High School Rodeo.

I went there in my truck, and there were three people from Williston with me. We were all laughing and joking around. As soon as I pulled in and parked, my mama ran to me and said, "Steve's been shot!"

I couldn't believe it. My spirits sank to the lowest they had ever been. Mama told me that Steve was out practicing with his 9mm when his show steer got out. He put the safety on, stuck the gun in the front of his pants, and ran after the steer, trying to get ahead of it. He tripped and the gun went off, knocking him for a complete flip.

The bullet blew away 2 inches of the main artery in his upper left leg, right near the groin. He actually bled to death on the way to the hospital, and he was also clinically dead twice from heart attacks.

When Steve was taken into the hospital the doctor said, "Give him blood immediately!"

The nurse asked, "What type?"

The doctor said, "It doesn't matter. He doesn't have any."

It was that bad.

Steve's dad later told me that when he put Steve into the back of his pickup truck and took off for the hospital, blood poured out of the back of the truck like water after a rain. He was first taken to the hospital in Palatka, and later transferred to Jacksonville.

It was over a month before I was allowed to see Steve, and when I went into his room he looked bad, but he was in good spirits. The doctors had told him he would never walk again, but he replied, "Oh yes I will!"

When I left the hospital I was in tears. Steve and I had been in rodeos together and we were like brothers. In fact, everyone I rodeoed with was family. That's the way it is on the rodeo circuit, but Steve and I were especially close.

Steve had told me many times that his one great desire was to win the championship buckle at his hometown rodeo, and now that dream was dead. He had looked forward to that rodeo all year. And then a thought struck me: I'll go there and win that buckle for Steve.

Before Steve got out of the hospital I went to his hometown rodeo in Palatka. I promised myself I would do my best to win this one for him, and I did. I took the buckle to Steve in the hospital and said, "Here ya' go, buddy. You won the buckle at your hometown rodeo. You might have been lying in this bed, but every bit of you was with me while I was riding that bull."

Steve's dad had ordered him an exact replica of the champion's buckle before I gave him the real thing. He never wore the replica.

And another miracle happened. After months of therapy and pain, Steve walked again – better than I did at that time. He not only survived all this, he proved the doctors wrong. He did this by sheer determination.

Chapter 10

Youthful
Folly &
More

Before going to Pueblo I went back to Frontier Town. The first morning there was spent unloading my truck and taking stuff up to the bunkhouse. On my second trip down to the truck, Jennifer was standing there. I almost fell down. She was prettier than I remembered. She still had that long curly hair and that beautiful face. I don't remember what she was wearing. All I could do was look at her face. We said a simple hello to each other, then she said, "We're going over to the Hitchin' Post to eat and play pool. Want to join us?"

I said, "We'll be over in a few minutes, as soon as we finish this."

The "we" was a rodeo buddy of mine from Florida, Keith Buchanan, who had come with me to work at the park. After only two weeks he left for home. He was homesick.

After unloading the truck, Keith and I went over to

the Hitchin' Post, a restaurant/bar across the street from the park entrance. We hadn't eaten yet so we went to the bar and ordered food. Jennifer was playing pool with Eddie.

As soon as I finished eating I went over to the jukebox and played "You Look So Good In Love" by George Strait. Jennifer stopped right in the middle of a shot, looked up, and started listening to the song; then she turned to me and asked, "Did you play that?"

I just grinned.

Later, we all went back to Frontier Town. Jennifer and I were sitting on one of the picnic tables making small talk. I finally said, "I know you've got a boyfriend, but I really wish you would give me another chance."

She said, "You know, you didn't even kiss me when you got here. Why don't you do it now?"

I did.

When the kiss was over, Jennifer said, "I think I know what to do."

As bad as I wanted to ask her what she meant by that, I didn't.

The next two days were nerve racking for both of us, but Jennifer finally told me she had broken up with her boyfriend. We started dating again, and we were both really happy.

We talked about Jennifer coming back to Florida with me to meet my Mom and Dad. She asked her parents about this, and all they said was "Whatever."

This was in the middle of the summer, and later, when it came time to leave, her parents had – let's say – a change of heart.

In mid-summer I flew to Pueblo for the High School Finals. Steve had ridden out there with his parents from Florida just to watch. I didn't do well in the rodeo, but it made me happy to see Steve doing so well after all he had been through. As I said, he was a walking miracle.

When the High School Finals ended, Steve flew with me back to Frontier Town. He was to take Keith Buchanan's place. I was glad, because we always had a lot of fun together.

As Steve's birthday approached, he begged me to let him ride a steer for his birthday present. The doctors had told him if he ripped that artery again he would die, so I kept telling him no – but he kept asking. Finally, on his birthday, I gave in and said, "Okay, but if you feel any strain on that groin, get off immediately. Please!"

He did just that, thank God. He rode the steer for a few seconds and then jumped off without any injury.

Now back to Jennifer and her parents' change of heart. The day before we were supposed to leave for Florida I went to see Jennifer in Salisbury. She was at a skeet shoot. Everything was still a go for her to go with me. She told me she would call me about 9 o'clock to make final plans. I gave her the number of a pay phone at the park.

That night I drove my truck to the end of the park where the phone was. I waited and waited and waited, but the phone did not ring. I finally fell asleep.

The next morning, when I woke up in my truck, I wondered why she didn't call, so I went back to the skeet shoot. She was there, and she explained to me what her dad had done: he ripped out the phone cord so she couldn't call me, then he took the license plates off her car so she couldn't drive it. When I heard this, I left there and went straight to her house. I knew her dad would be there.

Jennifer's dad hated me, and I was aware of that, so you can imagine his surprise when he opened the door and there I stood. I asked him if we could talk, and he invited me in.

We sat on a couch, and I said, "Why don't you want Jennifer to go to Florida with me?"

He replied, "I don't think it's in her best interest."

I shrugged and said, "If that's what you think."

I thanked him for his time and left.

Chapter 11

The
Escape

I went straight back to Frontier Town to pack my stuff and leave for Florida. As I was packing, I took down some pictures I had tacked on the wall and put them into my suitcase. They were pictures of Jennifer and me together in happy times. Tears came to my eyes. I said to myself, "If she wants to go with me, then dammit, she's going to!"

I left the bunkhouse and went across the street to the Hitchin' Post where Steve was having dinner. Together we devised a plan for the escape, as we called it. Then we went back to Salisbury to the skeet shoot.

Jennifer had just finished up, so she jumped in my truck. On the way to her house we explained the plan to her, and she liked it. When we reached her house we both got out of the truck so we could be seen if anyone was watching. Jennifer hugged me, like this was a final good-bye, then she ran in the house and did one heck of an acting job.

Jennifer started crying her heart out, then she said to her mom and dad, "I hope you're happy! He's gone now!"

She then ran up to her bedroom, but she didn't go there to cry on her pillow. She was packing.

Steve and I went to a Clint Eastwood movie, "Tight Rope," and after the movie, we headed back to Jennifer's house. We got there right on time – about ten minutes to midnight. The plan was for me to park my truck in a field down from her house, then Steve and I would sneak up to the back of the house where Jennifer's bedroom was located. She would lower her clothes and other stuff down to us with a rope, then she would walk out the front door, like she was just going for a walk to ease her sorrow. That was the plan, but a few things went wrong. It almost turned into a "Keystone Kops" flick.

Just as I parked the truck a drunk man came along in an old ice-cream truck with no muffler. It was loud. The man stopped and asked if I was having car trouble, and I assured him we were fine – just enjoying the night.

That old truck was loud when he was sitting there with the engine idling, but when he took off, it was really loud. There were only a few houses in that neighborhood, but I thought the noise from the truck would wake everybody for a mile around. Everyone would rush outside to see what was happening.

Nothing happened, so we continued with the plan. As we sneaked around to the back of her house, I noticed a clothes-line there, but in all the excitement, I must have forgotten about it.

Jennifer lowered down the first load. I had a suitcase in each hand, a pillow under one arm, and a big blanket under the other. I took off running across the yard, the same way we had come, and I hit that clothes-line in full stride. It would have knocked me down, but all that weight I was carrying held me upright, swaying like a pine tree in a high wind. I did get a black eye out of it, but I didn't make that same mistake on the second trip.

After Steve and I got everything loaded I ran back to her house to meet her, but I didn't get very far. She met me about fifty yards from her house. I hugged her, then we all got in my truck and headed out for Florida.

Looking back, I don't believe either one of us realized what a drastic step we were taking. We were two young people in love, and that's all that mattered. And remember – we were both eighteen at the time.

Chapter 12

Home on the Range – For Awhile

Jennifer stayed with me and my parents for two weeks, but I must say, they were kinda surprised when I showed up at the door with Jennifer in tow. Mom fixed up the spare bedroom for her.

My parents took to her well. We've got a saying in our family, "If you ain't at home here, you should be at home." Both of my parents always did everything possible to make anyone feel welcome in our house.

Mama and Daddy both liked Jennifer, but Daddy aggravates everybody. He always thinks he's just joking around, but sometimes he goes too far. You have to know him to appreciate him and understand his ways. Jennifer gave back tit-for-tat in a fun way, and they became friends. Both my parents accepted Jennifer as part of my life because they could see that I loved her.

The greatest adjustment for Jennifer was our house. She was used to better accommodations. Her dad was a building contractor – you could put our whole house inside his house and almost throw in our barn too. Our house didn't have air conditioning or central heat, so she was uncomfortable. It is still hot in Florida at that time of year. Very hot.

Jennifer did call her parents and tell them she was fine, and they talked several more times during her stay.

We spent a lot of time riding horses together, and Jennifer enjoyed this. We would ride down to the Morriston Store, about 2 miles from our house, and we would go riding far out on the prairie. Jennifer even helped us pen the cattle and work them in the pen. She seemed to fit right in with the kind of life we lived.

We also went into Williston and Ocala a few times, but most of our time was spent on horses. Although Jennifer wasn't too happy with the accommodations, she seemed happy to be with me. If she had regrets, it didn't show.

I didn't go to any rodeos during that month, for there were none close by. They were all in Mississippi and Arkansas, and at that stage in my rodeo career, I didn't usually go that far to participate.

The first part of October I took Jennifer to Savannah, Georgia for the World Skeet Shoot. She was chosen to be a referee, and that's a pretty big deal – there would be referees from all over the United States. She was proud to be chosen. We were also meeting her parents there. Her dad was one of the top skeet shooters in the nation, and he would be a participant.

As far as meeting her parents was concerned, I was pretty scared, especially when I thought about how we sneaked out of her house at midnight. When we finally got there, her mom and dad were surprisingly nice. I stayed with them for most of that day.

I'll never forget one thing that happened: Jennifer's

mom said to her, "Your dad and I are going canoeing tomorrow in the Okeefenokee Swamp."

That perked up my ears, and I guess a part of my dad's joking nature came out in me. I pointed to a canoe they had brought with them and said, "If you're going in that thing, you'd better have good life insurance. This ain't Maryland. We've got gators down here longer than that canoe, and they'll tip that thing over and eat both of ya'll."

Her mom's face turned deathly white. She turned to her husband and said, "Oh, honey, maybe we shouldn't go."

I had to choke back the laughter, and I'm sure Jennifer's dad could have swatted me with a stick.

Jennifer stayed with her parents for the skeet shoot, and I headed back to Florida alone. Each time I thought about that look on her mother's face, I laughed out loud. I don't know if they made that canoe trip or not.

Chapter 13

Back to Rodeo – & More

I'd bought my P.R.C.A. permit in August, but I didn't enter any rodeos until October. The weekend after I'd taken Jennifer to Savannah I went to the first of two rodeos I'd entered. The first, in Sumter County, was a smaller rodeo, meaning there was only $500 added. I drew a bull that was about three days older than Moses, and he didn't buck very well. I was only 57 points, but I got a little day-money.

In professional rodeo, when you pay your entry fees, half goes in the pot for the whole rodeo, including the $500 that's added. Half goes in the day-money pot, and this is split between the guys who make qualified rides that day. Example: if your fees are $50, $25 goes in the pot for the whole rodeo, which is paid to the guys who place; and $25 goes in the day-money pot. If there are fifteen riders that day, there would be $375 in the pot. If only one guy makes a qualified ride, he gets it all. If more than one rider qualifies, the money is split equally.

The next night I was in Bonifay for the largest rodeo in North Florida. There was $1500 added there, so my fees were $100. I'd drawn bull #6. When I asked the stock-contractor about him, he looked at me kinda sheepishly and said, "He's not very good."

I said to myself, "Great! My first two professional rodeos, and I draw two worthless bulls." But when I bought my permit, I said I just wanted to get my bulls ridden.

When I got a look at #6 he was pretty small. He had a black body and a white head. I didn't like small bulls even though I am very short myself. When #6 got in the chute, I set my rope and waited for my turn. When they came to me, I sat down on him and someone pulled my rope for me. I slid up and got a good seat, then I nodded for them to open the gate. When they did, #6 immediately started spinning to the left, and about half-way through the ride, he spun to the right. When the whistle blew, I jumped off and they announced my score: 72 points! That was currently second place.

I ended up in third place, but I won a little over $1100. I was on cloud nine! This win was important in a lot of ways, but the most important was that it takes $2500 to fill a permit and then be eligible to buy your P.R.C.A. card – then you're a member. Until then, a permit just allows you to enter P.R.C.A. rodeos.

After that weekend, I went back to Savannah to see Jennifer and tell her about my success. She was excited for me. She said, "I'm going back home with my parents, but they said I could drive back down to Florida later." I said, "Great," although I did have doubts. I remembered how her dad was. But a week later she did drive back to Florida.

During this second visit we were happy, I thought. We went to a couple of rodeos together in November. On the way to a rodeo in Brooksville, I said to her, "If I win the bullriding, will you marry me?"

She smiled and said, "Yes."

I was thrilled, and I was once again riding way up there on cloud nine. I promised myself that the ride in Brooksville would be my greatest ever, even if my bull weighed ten tons.

Well, what do you know – I drew the same bull I'd won the Ocala rodeo on when I was sixteen. He'd grown up a lot and was now much bigger, but I rode him again and won the bullriding. As soon as I raced to her in the stand, I said to Jennifer, kinda breathlessly, "I'm going to hold you to your promise!"

She gave me that melting smile and said, "O.K."

In December Jennifer said she wanted to go home and spend Christmas with her family. I said sure, so she left and drove north alone. I would never try to keep her from her family, even if it meant missing Christmas together.

Just before Christmas I sold my 1985 championship saddle – for two of the dumbest reasons, now that I look back and think about it. First, I had to have enough money to go to Maryland to see Jennifer; second, I bought her an engagement ring. It wasn't much, just a silver band with some diamond chips. They might not have even been diamonds for all I know. But it was silver. Jennifer liked silver, not gold. So on December 31st I took off for Maryland.

I arrived there the next day, January 1, 1989. Jennifer was at work at a toy store, so I went straight there. We hadn't seen each other in almost a month. She led me into an empty stall where we hugged and kissed each other, then I left to go to her friend's house and get some rest.

We met at the house later, and that's when I gave her the ring. Like I said, the ring wasn't much, but when I gave it to her, I gave it with more love than the biggest diamond ever pulled from the earth.

A couple of days later I left for home. I stopped in

Virginia, called her and said, "If you say the word, I'll turn this truck around and come back right now."

She said, "No, don't do that. Go on home. I'll join you there as soon as I have enough money."

I returned to our home in the country and waited for her, however long that would be.

Lake City, FL. 1988. Pee Wee riding #56. A bull owned by Guerney Geiger. Photo: Mike Rastelli

Chapter 14

Bumps
in
the
Road

On February 13, 1989 I received a letter from Jennifer. It said a lot of things, but the most crushing thing I've ever heard, seen, or read was this line: "I don't love you anymore."

Those words didn't make any sense, but they brought tears to my eyes. I could not imagine what had happened to make her write that. It was beyond my ability to comprehend.

I called Jennifer immediately and asked, "What does this mean? Is it something I have done?

She wouldn't talk about it. She just hung up the phone.

I had just gotten a good job managing a cattle ranch, which is a great opportunity for someone my age. The pay was good, and there was a house on the ranch they were going to give to me. This would be the first home for

Jennifer and me.

I pictured that house with a new white picket fence around it, lace curtains, and out back I would build a small barn with two stalls for our horses. There might also be a patio where we could sit in late afternoon and watch that dying Florida sky-ball sun bathe the prairie in a golden glow.

As soon as the money was available I would install central air/heat so Jennifer would be comfortable. Maybe I could even add a fireplace. Florida is known mostly for heat, but it can get very cold in the winter.

All of this was only in my mind, and it turned out to be no more than a pipe dream. After I got that letter, I went straight downhill.

I was so distracted by what had happened I was like a zombie in the saddle, my mind not even there, and that is a real no-no while working cattle. You have to be in full command of yourself, your reflexes perfect at all times. Just one slip, one lapse of judgment, could end in disaster. I knew I was in trouble, but the depressions wouldn't let up.

It came to a head when I lost that job because of my problems, then I went through four months of pure hell. I went to a few rodeos, but bullriding is 80% mental, and I couldn't keep my mind on what I was doing. I did manage to win a little money, but I was far from the top of my game, and I knew it. It was like being sucked straight down in a whirlpool and being helpless to stop it.

June finally came, and it was time to go back to Frontier Town. I knew I would come face-to-face with Jennifer again, and I had mixed emotions about this.

The first night there I attended a party, a kind of "before-the-park-opens" party for employees. Jennifer was there too, and I asked her if we could talk alone. She said yes and followed me outside. I said to her, "Jennifer, you taught me how to love. Now teach me how to stop loving you, just as you have done with me."

She said, "I'm not going to talk to you about this."

And that was it. She left.

Almost every time we came in contact with each other that summer, we argued. It was beginning to look hopeless. I tried to occupy my time with things other than her.

One weekend I was going to Cowtown, New Jersey to the P.R.C.A. rodeo they have there every Saturday night. The rodeos there were usually only one night, but this weekend they were having a two-day rodeo. That means you get on two bulls and try to win money in the average.

That Saturday I didn't have anyone to go with me, and I never went to a rodeo alone. Jennifer was the only person with that day off, and she didn't have a skeet shoot to go to. I asked her if she would ride up with me, just in case something happened to me. If something did happen, and it was bad enough to go to the hospital, she could take my insurance cards to the hospital and then drive my truck back to Frontier Town if she wanted to. I said to her pleadingly, "Please, let's set our differences aside and try to be friends."

She agreed, and the next day we headed up to Cowtown. It wasn't a long drive, only 2-1/2 hours, and we just made small talk along the way.

When we got there she sat in the bleachers while I went behind the chute to see my bull and take my ride. My bull didn't buck very well, so he was easy to ride.

We were only going to be there that one day, so after I got my equipment put away in my rigging bag we got in the truck and headed back. Jennifer was tired, so I suggested she lie down, put her head in my lap and sleep. I had a little '88 Isuzu pickup, but it had room for her to get comfortable. She slept all the way. All during that drive back I was glad we had spent at least a peaceful day together – no arguments.

A couple of weeks later there was a rodeo at the big Tri-State Fair in Delaware and everyone at Frontier Town who could get the day off went to this one. It was a P.R.C.A. rodeo, so I entered it.

I drew a bull named Okeechobee, and from that name, I knew he came from Florida. Most of the bulls they had were Florida rejects, but Okeechobee was an older bull. All of the other bulls were young and would weaken pretty fast. Older bulls don't.

Once I got set on Okeechobee, I nodded for them to open the gate. He really blew hard out of the chute, but I was used to that, and it didn't really bother me. He jumped and kicked pretty hard, but again, he was like a practice bull to me. About this time during the ride a young bull would weaken, but Okeechobee bucked to the fence, then turned really hard to the left. I had to make a hard move with my upper body and my free hand, but I didn't think it was a big deal. When I stepped off, they announced my score: 74 points!

Everyone behind the chutes thought that was one of the greatest rides they'd ever seen. I said to myself, "You northern boys better not come to a rodeo in Florida. Most of the bulls there really buck."

Everyone from Frontier Town came to me and congratulated me for winning the bullriding. I felt like my old self again. After everyone cleared out, Jennifer came up, gave me a big hug, and congratulated me. She knew that the money I'd won there filled my permit, and I could now buy my P.R.C.A. membership card. But I didn't do that right away – I waited until the next year. Another sideline to that day: everyone from Frontier Town wondered if Jennifer had come back to me.

Jennifer and I did become pretty good friends. That summer she lived in the "kitchen-trailer," a single wide trailer where the kitchen workers lived. The trailer was temporary home to Scott and Cathy, who owned the kitchen part of the Golden Nugget Saloon, and three other girls.

Some nights everyone would be partying in my bunkhouse, and I'd go over to the trailer and ask Jennifer if I could sleep there with her. She would say yes, but nothing serious would happen.

We went out on dates a couple of times. One night we went to the boardwalk in Ocean City. We had just ridden a terrifying ride – at least it was for me – but Jennifer couldn't stop laughing at me. I was as pale as a ghost. As we walked along, I saw one of those picture booths. I stopped and said, "I've never had my picture taken in one of those."

Jennifer said, "Well, then, let's do it."

I paid the money, then we got into the booth. It was so small Jennifer had to sit on my lap. The first two pictures were pretty normal – you know, just sitting and smiling. Then Jennifer leaned down and kissed me – that was the next three pictures. It was also the sweetest kiss I've ever had.

There wasn't much discussion about that kiss, but somehow we both knew it meant something. The next couple of days were kinda strange – close one moment, far apart the next.

That weekend was the time for our annual boat cruise. Everyone who worked at Frontier Town got on our boss's fishing boat, which was a large commercial fishing boat. We'd go up the coast to Delaware, then turn around and cruise back to Ocean City. It was about a 5-hour trip. We'd all dance and tell stories about each other, about things that had happened over the summer. A few of us guys were arm-wrestling on the back of the boat when someone started playing George Strait songs. I couldn't help myself. I went over to Jennifer and asked her if she wanted to dance.

She said yes. The water was like glass, and the boat wasn't rocking, so it was easy to dance. We seemed to have a good time together.

The next day I left alone for Florida. I had entered the rodeo in Ocala again.

Davie, FL., 1989. Pee Wee blasts out of the chute on bull #333. "I did the day money drag with this bull." Photo: Mike Rastelli

Chapter 15

New
Job
in
Delaware

It's about a 16-hour drive from Frontier Town to my home in Florida, but I ran into bad weather, and it took me longer. The next day was the rodeo in Ocala. I'd drawn an old bull, but he bucked really good. I tied for first three ways, but again I got the buckle.

I was off to a good start in rodeo, and I thought things between Jennifer and myself were settled, so I was feeling pretty good. A couple of weeks later it changed.

Jennifer sent me a letter. Among other things, she said that she still loves me. I was happy and mad at the same time. I couldn't believe that after all she'd put me through, she was really still in love with me. I was steamed. But I did find out that her dad threatened to take her out of his will if she married me.

Like an idiot, I did everything I could to get a job up there and be close to Jennifer, but there are no jobs available in Ocean City in the winter, especially for rodeo performers.

In October, at a rodeo in Gainesville, I had just ridden my bull and was winning the bullriding. A man approached me, introduced himself as Terry, and said he owned a company in Delaware that did cable TV installation and also tore down old systems. He said he was impressed by my performance, and he offered me a job.

My first reaction was, "Why me?" Why would a total stranger offer me a job in Delaware? I knew nothing about him or his business, but then it struck me: Delaware is only 2 hours from Jennifer. I said great, and accepted.

Unfortunately, with everything I'd gone through with Jennifer, I neglected my truck payments and the truck was repossessed. I had no transportation.

In early November we left for Delaware in Terry's truck. As soon as we arrived, I called my friend at Frontier Town, T.J., and asked him if he was interested in working in Delaware, that Terry would give him a job too. T.J. had stayed for awhile after the park closed, and there was nothing for him to do there, so he accepted without hesitation. He drove up and met me the next day.

On our first week-end off we drove down to Frontier Town to have a little party there with friends and to also see Jennifer. We all had a good time, then Jennifer said she had to go home early. I drove her there, and when I leaned over to kiss her goodnight, she pushed me away and said, "I'm seeing someone." Then she got out of the car and ran into the house.

I was confused. Just two months ago she said she was still in love with me. What the heck had changed? I called her a few times after that, but she wouldn't talk to me.

The work in Delaware turned out to be interesting, and I liked it. I learned how to climb telephone poles and install cables and do all kinds of stuff related to television. The only problem was the pay. T.J. and I lived in a motel, and by the time we paid the rent, there wasn't much left.

In late December we came back to Florida for Christmas. In early January '90 I entered my first Southeastern Circuit Finals. I hadn't been on a bull in more than three months, so I was pretty nervous. When you go from getting on bulls every weekend to nothing, you get rusty and lose your edge. But I had to try. I was listed in 12th place, which is the last place, but I'd made it.

In the first go-round I won 2nd. In the second go-round I rode my bull but didn't place, but that put me high in the average.

The third go-round I drew the "bucking bull of the year," so I had a great shot to win the average. If you win the average you get to go to the National Circuit Finals in Pocatello, Idaho and compete with all the other circuit and average winners. There are twelve circuits in P.R.C.A.

I had never seen this bull before, so I approached him with caution. Everybody said he really bucks. I eased on him, then another friend of mine, Audie Stokes, pulled my rope. I slid up and nodded for the bull to be released.

That bull blew out really hard, then he turned back to the right. I lost my seat when the bull turned back and was hanging off to the left, then he threw his head back to the left and knocked me out. I came loose from him and hit the ground.

When I regained somewhat consciousness the bull's head was right in my lap. I was out for only a few seconds and hadn't gotten all of my senses back, but when he turned away from me I rolled towards the bucking chute just in time to keep him from stepping on me with his back feet, which would have probably killed me. I was dazed for about thirty minutes, but I was all right.

We went back to Delaware for a while, but things just

got worse. Terry didn't pay us much to begin with, and he never increased it. We couldn't get by on what we were making. Luckily I'd saved some of the money I'd won at the finals, so T.J. and I got in his car and came back to Florida.

On the way back something happened that was kinda funny. We got a flat tire somewhere in Maryland, and when a state trooper pulled up behind us, we asked him if he would help us. We explained to him that we didn't have a spare, so if he would drive one of us to town to buy a tire, it would surely be a big favor. He said he would have to search our car first.

You should have seen the look on his face when I opened my rigging-bag. I tried to explain all the equipment to him, but he just shook his head and said, "Forget it, man. It's not a bomb or a weapon, so you're O.K." The whole time he was laughing – then he did us that favor and took T.J. to town for a new tire, and also brought him back.

We arrived home in late February. T.J., being from Pennsylvania, had never worked cattle or done anything of that nature, so he really enjoyed doing this with us. It was a new adventure for him.

By then I had bought my P.R.C.A. card, but I bought it for the First Frontier Circuit up north. About that time I got hooked-up with Bud Connolly, who once worked with Daddy, and we went to a lot of rodeos together, all of them in the Southeastern Circuit. Bud was originally from Minnesota and his wife is from Florida.

In just three months I won over $2000, which to me was a lot of money.

In early April, T.J. and I decided to go up to T.J.'s home in Pennsylvania so he could spend some time with his family. We would go from there down to Frontier Town in June. T.J. went back on a bus because Bud and I had a rodeo in Tennessee. We would meet T.J. later at a rodeo in

Lake Erie, Pennsylvania. I was driving T.J.'s car, a Chevrolet Spider, which is very low to the ground.

At the rodeo in Tennessee I won 3rd and Bud got thrown off, so we headed for Pennsylvania that night. We got tired and stopped for the night at a motel, and when we awoke the next morning it was 9:30. We were about 300 miles from Lake Erie and had to be there at 7 p.m., so we dressed in a hurry and took off. T.J.'s car was not exactly speedy, but I pushed the pedal to the metal and we got there at 7:10. Bud drew a good bull and won the bullriding. I rode my bull but didn't place.

The next day Bud flew back home, and T.J. and I headed to his house in Beaver County, which is about an hour and a half from Pittsburgh. His family really treated me nice. We kicked around his hometown for about a month, then we headed down to Frontier Town.

It was two weeks before the park would open, but we went early to help get the park ready for opening day. I mainly wanted to see Jennifer and find out if she was now available.

She wasn't.

Chapter 16

Frontier
Town
1990

Jennifer still had a boyfriend. I'll just refer to him as Jerk. At first I didn't like him because he had Jennifer and I wanted her. But jealousy soon turned to rage.

I still went to Cowtown on weekends, but my new girlfriend, Jenny, had gotten a ticket for me to go to the Aerosmith concert in Virginia. A lot of people from Frontier Town were going there, but I learned that Jennifer and Jerk were going too.

Tensions were pretty high between Jerk and me because of my jealousy, so everyone asked me not to go. I said fine, I'll just go to Cowtown instead. And I did.

The next day, Sunday, a lot of people who went to the concert told me that Jennifer was up dancing when Jerk grabbed her, threw her down in her chair, and screamed at her. Then she cringed like she was expecting him to hit her.

That told me that he had hit her before, because a child isn't afraid of a dog until they've been bitten.

When I heard this I promised that if I ever saw Jerk again I'd put him in a lot of pain. Nobody was going to treat Jennifer that way. Nobody! She is too good a person for that. She didn't love me anymore, but that didn't matter.

The next time I saw Jennifer I told her to never bring Jerk to Frontier Town again. She bristled, and then she said, "I'll bring him here if I want to!"

This was near the end of the summer season, and that's when a big restaurant in Ocean City, Harrison's, rents the park for one night for their employees. They rent the park from 6:30 until whenever they want to leave. We put on a couple of shows for them, and after that, we were allowed to join the party if we wanted to. They have the food catered, and it's always great.

By 9:00 I was back in my bunkhouse. T.J. came in and said, "Jennifer and Jerk just got here."

The rage was still there, so I went outside looking for Jerk. When I found him I walked right up to him and said, "I would like to talk to you. Let's go behind this building."

Jerk was much bigger than me, 5'10" and 200 pounds, almost twice my weight, but I didn't care. When we got back there, he spread his arms, grinned, and said, "Hit me."

I said, "You've got to be kidding."

Before I could say anything else he swung at me. I stepped towards him so he'd miss, then we started wrestling around on the ground. First thing I knew he had me pinned, but I grabbed his wrists so he couldn't hit me.

Jerk then started laughing at me, and that really ticked me off. I let go of his wrists and started punching him in the face as hard as I could. I was pretty darn strong, and after I had hit him multiple times, I grabbed his wrists again and lay there resting from my flurry.

When my eyes focused again, I noticed that Jerk was bleeding from his nose and mouth. He shifted his weight, laughed again and said, "This is really stupid and funny. Have you had enough?"

I laughed too and said, "Sure. Whatever."

After this little tussle I walked a short distance away and realized my shirt had blood all over it. Since this was supposed to be a fight, not a wrestling match, I figured I had won.

After that Jennifer really hated me. I knew she didn't deserve to be treated that way – no woman does – but if they stay in a situation like that, it's their problem.

A month after I had returned home from Frontier Town, one of my friends up there told me that Jennifer married Jerk. I said to myself, "If that's the way she wants to live, so be it. It's her mistake."

So begins a new chapter in my life.

Chapter 17

1991
& More
Bumps

After I left Frontier Town in September '90 I didn't have a job for about two months. I went to amateur rodeos and won just enough money to get by.

At the end of November '90 I met a guy named John at a rodeo. He was from Pennsylvania but was working in Florida. I told him about me being without a job and he said, "There's a guy where I work who's about to quit. If you want, I'll get you that job."

I had never been without a steady job for that long, so I said, "Great. I'll take it."

Turns out the job was on a thoroughbred horse farm, and I hate thoroughbreds. They're crazy. But it was a job, and we wouldn't have much contact with the horses except to feed them. Most of our time would be spent doing farm maintenance, such as mowing the grass, repairing fences, and moving dead trees out of the paddocks.

John was looking for a new place to live, so I invited him to live with me and my parents, rent-free. He thought this was great, and he accepted.

This was in late November '90. John was also a bullrider, so we lived, worked, and rodeoed together, becoming close friends, almost like brothers. I won more rodeo money than John, but that didn't bother him. We had great fun together.

In July '91 I won the W.W.R.A. for the most money received by any rider in that association for the whole season. W.W.R.A. stands for World Wide Rodeo Association, but it's really not world wide. It's just North Florida and South Georgia. It's a small amateur association, but I also won a saddle. In '91 I hadn't yet renewed my P.R.C.A. card, so I could only go to amateur rodeos, but they were fun.

John went back home to Pennsylvania in early August. When he returned at the end of October, he had a new Mazda pickup truck.

During his absence, a lot of things happened to me.

In September a friend of mine from Chiefland – his name is David – went with me to a Labor Day rodeo in Dade City. We were scheduled to ride on Sunday, but we went on Saturday just to watch. We had friends there too, so we went to a party with them after the rodeo.

I was twenty-one by that time, so we all went to a bar and had a few beers. That's bad enough, but then I did something really stupid. I borrowed David's truck to go get something to eat.

I got lost, and then I got pulled over by the police. They smelled beer on me and arrested me for DUI. I spent 7 hours in jail before my dad could get the money for bail. That was the first time, and the last time, that happened to me, and I don't recommend it to anyone.

I've never experienced fear like that. The people running the jail kept moving me around so I wouldn't be subjected to hardened criminals, but that didn't help. I shook the whole time I was in there. I knew I couldn't just get up and leave that jail, that I was trapped like a coon in a steel cage, and that's a terrible feeling. It taught me a lesson I never forgot.

John got back a week before my court date. The next night Taco and I went with him in his new truck to Williston to play pool. Then Taco said, "Why don't we go to this place in Ocala? We can have fun there too."

John said fine. I wasn't so hot on the idea, especially in light of my current troubles, but I reluctantly agreed.

When we reached John's truck outside, Taco and I argued over who would have to sit in the middle. I won, and I got the seat next to the door. It was very hot, so we had the windows down, and that could have saved my life.

On the way to Ocala we came upon a semi-truck with a flat-bed trailer parked across the whole road, with all of its lights off. There was a car just ahead of us, and when he saw the trailer it was too late. He slammed on his brakes but hit the trailer.

John slammed on his brakes too, but we hit the tires of the trailer head on. We all hit the windshield and it broke away. The only thing that kept me from flying out and smashing head-on into the truck body was that I grabbed the door and hung on for dear life. If we hadn't had those windows down I wouldn't have had anything to grab, and I hate to think what could have happened to me.

John and Taco were just shook-up, but I suffered a broken right foot. The break wasn't bad, and I was on crutches for only three weeks. I was still working at the thoroughbred farm, but I lost that job because I couldn't work with a broken foot and they needed someone on the job every day.

When my time came, I had to go to court on crutches. The judge gave me 50 hours of community service, a $2500 fine, probation, and the loss of my driver's license for six months. The probation was to end as soon as the fine was paid – which I paid that day – and the community service completed.

The next weekend I went to Chiefland to practice as best as I could with a broken foot. My friend Gene had some practice bulls at his house and a makeshift arena everyone called "the dungeon." When I arrived they already knew about my DUI because David was there and he had told them. They all laughed at me, especially Billy.

Billy is David and Gene's cousin. He really thought it was funny, but a week later he got a DUI too, and then it wasn't so funny. He was only nineteen at the time, but he got almost the exact punishment as I did. When he went to court the judge asked him, "Son, do you know what you did wrong?"

Billy said, "Yes, sir. I shouldn't have been drinking and driving."

The judge glared at him and said angrily, "No, son, you shouldn't have been drinking at all. You're only nineteen!"

Billy didn't laugh.

Billy and I did our community service together. We helped the Kiwanis Club clean up the grounds for their rodeo in Chiefland. We also helped set up the arena and the bleachers, and we had fun doing it.

We were both entered in the rodeo, and I won 3rd place and a little money. I guess you could say, in a way, I got paid for my community service.

Chapter 18

Here
Comes
Molly

After all of that was over, John and I started working together on another horse farm, and we lived together again. One day John got a call from a girl he had once dated a couple of times back in Pennsylvania. Her name was Julie. She asked John if she could come down to Florida to see him. John knew that Julie liked him, but he didn't feel the same way about her. He was not the type of guy who could ever be rude to anyone, so he said sure.

A few days later Julie showed up here. She stayed with us in the spare bedroom. As I said, John was not a rude guy, but knowing how she felt about him, he wasn't especially nice either. I can make friends with almost anyone, so I was nice to her. She stayed three days and then went back to Pennsylvania.

We both thought that was the end of it, but a couple of months later, in early November, she called again. I answered the phone, and Julie asked me if she could come back down again. Then she said, "I've got someone who wants to meet you. Her name is Molly. She saw the pictures I took while I was down there, and she likes what she sees."

I wasn't really listening, so I just said, "That's cool."

Molly then came on the phone and said, "We'll be down there Thursday." And that was the end of the conversation.

They had already arrived when John and I came home from work that Thursday. When we walked into the house I first noticed Julie sitting on one end of the sofa, then I glanced to the right and saw this beautiful blonde sitting next to her. I couldn't believe my eyes. She had long blonde curly hair and deep hazel eyes. She was wearing shorts, revealing long classy legs – like a thoroughbred's.

Both girls got up immediately, then Julie introduced us. I shook Molly's hand and said, "It's good to meet you." I turned to Julie and said, "I've got to talk to you alone in the kitchen – now!"

As soon as we were in the kitchen I said, "What the heck do you mean bringing such a beautiful girl down here to meet someone as ugly as me? She doesn't want to meet me! You just brought her to keep me occupied so John will pay more attention to you!"

Julie said, "No, that's not true. She really does want to meet you and spend time with you. And, besides, you're not ugly. You're kinda cute."

I brushed that last remark aside and continued staring at her. I still didn't believe it.

They stayed at the house for a half-hour, then they left for their motel in Gainesville, which is only thirty minutes from my house. As soon as they got there Julie called and asked John if we would come over. John still didn't like her so he said no.

Molly got on the phone and asked for me. She said,

"We really do want you two to come over, even if it's just for a little while."

John had already said no, and I respected that. We stayed home.

Julie and Molly planned to stay in Florida for eleven days. John and I had two rodeos during that time, one that Saturday and one the next Saturday. We went to the first one in Callahan, and the girls went with us. Neither one of us did good – we both got bucked off. The girls thought this was funny.

John was a good sport about all of this, mostly for my sake. He knew I was interested in Molly, and he didn't want to do anything to stand in my way. He just went along with it.

Later that week, we spent as much time as we could with the girls. One night when Molly and I were alone, she gave me a "kitten look" and said, "I love you."

I said it back, but as soon as the words came out of my mouth, I thought, "Why would such a beautiful girl who has known me only six days say such a thing?"

I found out a little later. It was unfortunate for two people. I am one of them.

Our next rodeo was an exhibition rodeo in Ocala. It was for a group of people from South America who were touring Florida.

We were scheduled to do all events in rodeo, but we did only four of each event. There were four calf ropers, four steer ropers, four barrel-racers, four bareback riders, four saddle bronco riders, and four bullriders.

The man in charge told us to pick any bull we wanted. The two other bullriders picked the two biggest bulls, then John picked the next biggest. That left me with the last bull, a small one.

I knew something about this bull. He was one of my old practice bulls that we had sold to a stock contractor. He could really buck, and he was fun to ride. The other guys hadn't picked him because he was so small.

After the other two guys and John had ridden – they all got bucked off – I came out on that little bull. He blew out like a storm, spinning both ways, first left and then right. When the whistle blew, I did this little thing I do (everybody does it now, but not back then) – I jumped off and threw my hat high into the air. Those people went crazy. They gave me a standing ovation, then they stomped their feet and kept screaming until it seemed to last forever.

After I'd put my stuff away several guys from Argentina came up to me and started jabbering in Spanish. I couldn't understand a word they were saying, but they offered me a shot of some kind of liquor they had brought with them from Argentina. There wasn't much left in the bottle because they had been drinking during the whole rodeo and were pretty drunk.   I said no thanks, then another guy and his wife motioned me over. I couldn't understand them either.

About that time a man named Peppi walked by. I'd known him for a long time and had rodeoed with his son in high school. Peppi was originally from Argentina, and he spoke Spanish as well as English. I asked Peppi what this man was saying. Peppi talked to him for a minute, then he said to me, "This guy was so impressed by you. He wants you to have his wife tonight."

As soon as he said that I took off running. I found Molly, brought her back with me, and said to Peppi, "Explain to this man that this is my wife, and we don't do that sort of thing in Florida."

As soon as Peppi explained it to him, the man apologized and left. I was glad that Molly and Peppi were there. If they hadn't been, I would have been in one heck of a mess.

Chapter 19

A
Twisting
Road
with
Molly

Julie and Molly left late the next day. Molly promised she would call me, and I thought yeah, right. I doubted I would see or hear from her again.

Over the next two months we did talk occasionally by phone. One day I called her and she said, "I can't talk right now."

In the background I heard a man's voice. I hung up and called Julie, and she told me Molly had a new boyfriend. I said thanks, bye, and hung up. I thought, "Well, that's that."

About two weeks later, in late January '92, Molly called and asked me if she could come down for a short visit. I said sure. Mom cleaned up the spare bedroom again.

She came down on a late Friday night. We didn't do much that whole weekend except talk. She left that Sunday, and again I thought, "This is it." Then in mid-February she called and asked if she could come down and spend a week or two. I asked my parents and they said yes. They liked Molly. So it was all set.

Molly arrived right on schedule. Mama got called away for awhile to take care of my grandma and grandpa, who weren't doing well, so Molly took over the housekeeping. She did pretty well at it --better than I expected.

We rode horses together some, but not much. This was after Black died, and I wasn't much into riding horses. I still had too many vivid memories of Black.

We talked a good deal, but no matter what the subject, it always came back to one thing – marriage. All Molly wanted to talk about was us getting married. It was like having a parrot in the house who could say only three words, "Let's get married." But I never said no. I went along with it. But each time I looked at her, I thought it was a great idea. I didn't get my hopes too high because I had already been burned badly by Jennifer. I didn't think I could go through something like that again.

She decided to extend the visit, so we had to go up to Pennsylvania to return her mother's car, which she had borrowed. Her mother then gave her a used '88 Ford station wagon.

From the first moment I met her mother, I could tell she thought I wasn't good enough for Molly. Most of the time she treated me as if I didn't exist.

We only stayed there a couple of days, and on the way back to Florida we stopped in Georgia, where I entered a rodeo. I won 2nd and got a pretty good pot, so it wasn't like we were always broke.

Molly talked to her mother quite often on the phone, and each time they talked her mother would say, "That boy isn't good enough for you."

After months of up-and-down jobs, I finally got a good job at the door-mill in Williston. Before that, rodeo was my main income, but amateur rodeos don't pay much. You've got to draw a good bucking bull to win money, and there aren't many good bucking bulls in amateur rodeo. Your chances are slimmer.

In case you don't know what a door-mill is, it's where pre-hung doors are made. You take a ready-made door that doesn't have a hole in it for the door knob or hinges, drill the hole, put the hinges on, then build a jam around it. When it gets to wherever it's going, to a construction or remodeling site, they just have to put it in the door opening, shim it up straight, and nail it in place. It was interesting work, and I enjoyed it.

I had been at my new job for only a week when my niece, Holly, went into the hospital with acute appendicitis. Molly picked me up at work to take me there. When she let me out at the hospital she said, "I'm going home to see my mom. I'm leaving now. I'll be back in a week."

This was quite a surprise. She hadn't mentioned it before then, but I said sure.

The next Friday I called her to make sure she was leaving for Florida the next day. She said that her grandfather was in the hospital and she would stay until he was all right. I said fine, and I assured her that I would never ask her to put me above her family.

The next Friday I called again to see if her grandfather was doing better and when she thought she'd be back. I had a surprise for her, an engagement ring. This time it was a real one, and I'd bought it with money I'd saved from my rodeo winnings. I thought I wanted to marry her, but a series of events changed my mind forever.

When I called that day, her mother answered the phone. I asked to speak to Molly, and her mother said, "Molly is getting married. Don't ever call here again!" Then she hung up.

I was devastated again, but this time I think my pride was hurt more than my heart. I think I was more in love with Molly's looks than with her. Jennifer was beautiful too, but I loved her as a person. I'm not sure it was that way with Molly.

I gradually dismissed all of this from my mind, and then six weeks later I got a call from Molly. She said she wanted to fly down and explain to me what had happened. I told her to come on down, that I'd really like to hear that.

That Thursday she flew into Gainesville. I took the day off so I could meet her at the airport. Her plane was scheduled to arrive at 9 a.m., but they had a delay in Atlanta and didn't arrive until 10:30. When she came into the terminal she was wearing tan shorts, a white shirt, and lots of jewelry. Her legs were deeply tanned. I knew the weather up in Pennsylvania wasn't warm enough yet for that, so she must have been in a tanning-bed or maybe down in the Caribbean.

We said hello, but there were no hugs or kisses. She didn't have any luggage because she would fly back later that day.

We sat on a bench in the terminal, then I said, "Okay, let's hear it."

First she said her mother made her marry this man because he has lots of money. He's twice her age, but he has a string of six video rental stores. Her mother forced her into it.

I said to her, "Aren't you the one who said 'I do?' Your mother couldn't say that for you."

At first she didn't know how to answer, then she said, "It's complicated. I really don't know how to explain everything."

I said, "Did you fly all the way down here just to tell

me what you've said so far? You could have done that on the phone."

"No, I wanted to face you and say I'm sorry," she said. "If I've hurt you, I didn't mean to. This is not the way I thought it would end. But it's over. We won't see each other again."

"So be it," I said. Then I got up and left.

All the way back home I thought about what had happened. I wondered what was wrong with me. Am I too short, too ugly? Am I just a dumb country hick who is out of his league except for a cattle ranch or a rodeo? Maybe I was just a temporary amusement for Molly and for Jennifer too, like one of those little wooden dummies on strings you can jerk about and then discard when you lose interest.

I finally said this to myself: If you have the same luck with bulls as you have with girls, you'll get your neck broken someday.

By then I had quit my door-mill job and was working on a cattle/hay farm, baling hay and loading it for customers. One day I went back to the door-mill to repay a loan the owner had given me. The foreman came to me and asked if I would come back to work there. He said they would start my probation from the day I'd quit, that I wouldn't have to start over. The benefits were good, and there was only a three-month probation period before your benefits were available. I had already worked there for two months, so that sounded great. I took the job.

A couple of weeks later I met Tracy. She is younger than me and shorter than me. At 4'11" I could look down into her eyes, which were a very pretty blue. She had medium length brown hair. Right from the start, Tracy and I got along fine. And besides that, we made a damn cute couple. I was introduced to her by a friend of mine, Joe, who had gone to school with Tracy.

At that time I'd almost quit riding bulls. One Saturday while Tracy and I were at Joe's apartment a friend of his came in and mentioned a little rodeo scheduled for that night in Lake County at the boy's ranch. He said that Leroy Mason was putting it on. I'd known Leroy since the P.R.C.A. rodeo in Ocala in '86, so I called him and asked if I could get in the bullriding that night. The call-in deadline was the Monday before, but Leroy made an exception for me. And besides, I wasn't exactly unknown in the rodeo world. He said sure, come on over.

Tracy went with me. The entry fee was only $25, so I didn't have much to lose. Then I won the bullriding. It paid only $150, but I'd spent only $10 for gas and $5 for drinks and hamburgers for Tracy and myself. I ended up making a profit of $110. After I was paid by the rodeo secretary, Leroy came up to me and said, "I'm going to have one of these events every other Saturday night for three months. If you'll help load the bulls in the chutes and flank them, I'll pay your entry fees."

This was a chance to get back into rodeo and make a little money too, so I said yes.

Chapter 20

**Back
to
Rodeo**

Orlando O'rena, 1993. Pee Wee riding the formidable bull H4 aka The Russian Sickle in an P.R.C.A. rodeo. Photo: Mike Rastelli

I entered a series of eight rodeos in July and August. I won six of them, placed 3rd in one, and didn't place in one, but I had more points than anyone else, so I won the series. I got a nice buckle. I thought to myself, "Maybe I've still got 'it'."

Leroy then told me he had two P.R.C.A. rodeos coming up in September, so I bought my P.R.C.A. card back. In September I went to my first P.R.C.A. rodeo in over a year. It was in Lakeland, and it turned out to be a two-header – that's when you get on two bulls. The first night I had a bull that was supposed to be easy to ride, but he threw me off. That really upset me, and I thought, "Maybe I don't have 'it' back."

The next day I had a bull that had gone unridden in thirty tries, but to me it was a challenge. When I got on him someone pulled my rope, then I slid up, got a good seat and nodded. He spun to the left in the gate, then he spun to the right. I jumped off when the whistle blew, and they announced my score: 76 points! I won 3rd in the average on just one bull. I said to myself, "I do have 'it' back!"

The next weekend the rodeo was in the Orlando O'rena. I was entered for Saturday night, and I'd drawn a really good bull: H4 The Russian Sickle. This bull had been to the National Finals in Las Vegas five times, and he was the bucking bull of the Southeastern Circuit about six times. Don't ask me why he was named The Russian Sickle. Stock contractors name their bulls all kinds of strange names. But I do know what a sickle can do to anything that gets in its way.

To face any bull, but especially a bull like this, you need your body rested, and I had a problem. On Friday night I stayed up all night with Tracy and her sick horse. The next morning I told her to stay at home and watch her horse, but she insisted on going to the rodeo. Three other friends went with us; Joe, J.J., and Beth.

At the time I was living with Beth, and I'd best explain this. She was a friend I'd known for a long time. She was 25 at that time and was living in a rental trailer. I wanted to move out of my parent's house, so Beth said if I would pay half the rent and utilities, I could live there. We just shared the trailer – that and nothing more. Needless to say, Tracy didn't think much of the arrangement. She was more than kinda jealous.

When we all arrived in Orlando at 10 a.m. we got a hotel room with two beds so we could rest before the rodeo that night. We rested for about 7 hours, but I didn't sleep. Here I was facing the bucking bull of the year, and no sleep for two days.

Later, when we reached the O'rena, all of our group went to buy their tickets and find their seats. I went behind the chutes to await my turn.

I guess the excitement and adrenaline were really kicking in, because all of a sudden I didn't feel tired at all.

When my turn came I got down on H4 and someone pulled my rope. I took my wrap, then I slid up, got a good seat and nodded. H4 went two jumps out and started spinning to the left really hard. I had to do everything I had ever known to stay on, but I rode him.

Just after the whistle blew, H4 threw me right on top of my head. I thought he'd broken my neck, but I was fine – more than fine. They announced my score: 86 points! I'd been close to 80 points before, but never this many points. It was also the only time I've ever known I would win the bullriding before the rodeo ended. There were more bullriders yet to come that night and the next day, but I had checked everyone's draw, and there were no more bulls that bucked better than mine.

I felt like I was on top of the world. All my friends congratulated me. After the rodeo ended, everyone except Tracy and me went to a bar to celebrate. Tracy was only 19 then, so we went back to the room to get some much-needed sleep.

The next morning Tracy called her mom to see how her horse was doing, and her mom said, "I'm sorry, Tracy, she died last night."

Tracy was devastated. She ran down to a little lake by our hotel and cried her eyes out. I sat next to her, and she cried on my shoulder. I didn't know what to say. I would never tell her she should have stayed home with her horse. I was still on cloud nine from the ride the night before, so I just sat with her and tried not to say much.

Later that day Tracy rode home with Beth and J.J. I stayed behind to get my check, and Joe stayed with me. I did win first in the bullriding and even got a buckle – some P.R.C.A. rodeos do give buckles too. But the whole thing was dimmed by Tracy's grief.

Chapter 21

1994

Athens, GA., April, 1994. Pee Wee riding Rudy Valle bull #01, Star. "I was only 74 points on him and didn't place." Photo: Mike Rastelli

Because I bought my P.R.C.A. card so late in 1993 I only went to one more rodeo that year. This one was in Bonifay, and I got thrown off. Before I knew it I had to renew my card again.

I started 1994 without someone to travel with, so I didn't go to many rodeos for the first three months of the year. Tracy couldn't go with me because she was in college at the University of Florida. I moved out of Beth's place because Tracy was giving me a lot of friction. She thought Beth and I had something going, but we didn't. I moved back in with Dad. Mom was still in Panama City taking care of her daddy. Grandma had passed away by then.

One day I was in Chiefland at the practice pen when I met Greg McManus. He had a nickname, Greg Mc – pronounced like Greg Mac – and since everyone called him that, I did too, and it just sounded kinda right.

Greg Mc was 25, a year older than me, and was

married to someone I knew, Janie. This was just before I moved back to Dad's house. One night Janie called me and said, "Why don't you and Greg Mc travel together?"

I said, "That sounds great."

Greg Mc then got on the phone and said, "Hey." And that was about it.

I said to Greg Mc, "Let's enter the rodeo next weekend in Clemson, South Carolina."

Greg Mc said, "O.K."

When I hung up I said to Beth, "That boy doesn't talk too much. I'm going to fall asleep traveling with him and no one to talk to."

The day we left for the rodeo we took Janie's car, and it wasn't long before we started talking, then we talked almost non-stop all the way to South Carolina. We found out we had a lot in common. Greg Mc was from Arkansas and had come down to Florida to marry Janie. I said, "That's nothing. I would have moved to Maryland a long time ago if things had worked out with a girl there. But they didn't."

We had a lot of other things in common too, and also had our differences – not personality wise, but in other ways. I started riding bulls when I was 14, and that's all I wanted to do since then. Greg Mc didn't start until he was 18. Two older guys who used to ride bulls got him interested in it, then Greg Mc started going to a practice pen close to his house. They had only steers that were too big to rope anymore – no bulls. Greg Mc said, "I couldn't ride good at all to begin with, but every weekend I couldn't wait to go down there just to get on one of those big steers."

Greg Mc and I went to a lot of rodeos together but they were mostly small rodeos in Florida and South Georgia. We were making a little money but not enough to call this a living, and Greg Mc had a family to support.

In late August Greg Mc said to me, "Why don't we try to make the Circuit Finals? There's good money there."

We looked at the standings: Greg Mc was 23rd, and I was sitting in 25th place. Only the top 12 go to the Finals. I said to Greg Mc, "There's no way."

He said, "There's a lot of big paying rodeos coming up. We'll just enter them."

"That suits me fine," I said.

We had a little setback coming home from one of those smaller rodeos, this one in Albany, Georgia. Part of it was funny to me, but yet not so funny.

We left home late that day for the rodeo, and I was driving. We had a rental car, so I was driving much faster than I would in my own vehicle. Fact is, sometimes I hit 100 miles per hour. I drove like an idiot, weaving in and out of cars but doing so as safely as possible. Greg Mc just held on to his hat and prayed, and we both wished we had left home earlier that day.

We barely made it to the rodeo in time, and it turned out that this wild trip was for nothing. Greg Mc rode his bull but didn't place in the money. I rode my bull, but about six seconds into the ride he stopped. That meant I got a re-ride, and this time the bull threw me off. We both came away with zero cash.

Now for the part that was funny, only to me. Greg Mc drove going back home, and along the way he passed a Georgia State Trooper sitting on the side of the road. He must have just finished writing someone else a ticket. Greg Mc passed him doing 70 miles an hour in a 55 mile per hour zone. The trooper immediately got behind us and turned on his blue lights. Greg Mc said, "You reckon he's after me?"

I said, "Yes, he's after you. You just passed him doing 70."

Greg Mc didn't stop until he was 5 miles down the road, and he didn't slow down either. He finally said, "I guess he is after me."

That's when I had to laugh, remembering I'd clocked 100 earlier that day along this same stretch and had gotten away with it.

When Greg Mc finally pulled over and stopped, the trooper came to our car and said to him, "Didn't you see me behind you?"

Greg Mc said, "Yeah, but I didn't think you were after me."

The trooper said, "I clocked you at 70. Who did you think I was after? Why didn't you slow down and stop?"

Greg Mc said, "Well, I didn't want to look suspicious."

At that point I couldn't help myself – I snickered. The trooper looked at me strangely and asked to see my ID, then he issued Greg Mc a ticket and told him to mail the fine back just as soon as we got home to Florida.

Since we didn't win any money, that little rodeo in Albany turned out to be a financial disaster.

Although we weren't in the big money, Greg Mc and I were having a lot of fun. Some weekends we would go to two different rodeos, and they might be 150 or 200 miles apart. We'd leave on a Friday afternoon and wouldn't get back home until late Sunday night.

Janie went with us sometimes because she doesn't work. She and Greg Mc had two children, a daughter, Kirsten, 4, and a son, Cord, who was 1 year old. The kids would go along too, and I thought this was cool. I got along great with those kids, and I really enjoyed having them with us.

Tracy could never go with us because she was in

college and couldn't miss her Friday classes. This often made her feel like an outsider, especially when Janie went along. Unfortunately, I couldn't see this at the time. This was the greatest time of my rodeo career, and I was having the time of my life. I didn't realize how much Tracy wanted to share this with me.

Daytona, 1994. Pee Wee just out of the chute on Castaway, a bull owned by Rudy Valle. He scored 74 points & took 3rd place. Photo: Mike Rastelli

Our first big rodeo was in Memphis, Tennessee in early September. The Circuit Finals are in November, and Greg Mc and I were still far behind.

I promised Tracy she could go with us to Memphis. Janie couldn't go because it was too long a trip for the kids. Greg Mc nor Janie knew that Tracy was going until the Friday we left. Greg Mc didn't mind, but Janie was mad about it. I didn't really care what she thought. I had promised Tracy she could go, and that was it.

Greg Mc and I weren't up until Saturday night, but because it was such a long trip, we left early Friday afternoon so we could stop along the way and get some rest. I had rented a car for the trip. I had done that all year because a car gets better mileage than a truck and if it breaks down along the way you don't have to shell out your own money to get it fixed. The rental company just brings you another car.

That night we stopped at a motel and all they had left was a single room with a double bed. I usually sleep right on the edge of a bed and hate sleeping in the middle, but that night I slept between Tracy and Greg Mc. I was so tired I didn't really care.

The next morning we all got up, took turns taking showers, and went to a Shoney's restaurant across the street for breakfast. We didn't even know where we'd stopped for the night until we asked the waitress. She said, "Ya'll are in Tupelo, Mississippi, honey."

That meant we weren't far from Memphis, so we could take our time and not drive fast for a change.

Chapter 22

Weird
Ride
in
Memphis

W̲e took our time going on to Memphis and passed through some really pretty country in North Mississippi. Lots of pines and hickory and magnolia trees. There were also towns with interesting names, like New Albany, Myrtle, Hickory Flat, Potts Camp, Holly Springs, Red Banks, and Olive Branch. When you're on the rodeo circuit you sometimes wish you could stop along the way, meet the people and see the local sights, but you can't. You have to push on, and you miss a lot of things along the way. I guess it's the same with those groups who play the music circuit.

The rodeo performance started at 8 that night, and we reached the fair grounds at 1 p.m. We didn't realize how big this place was until we saw it. It was a huge – and I mean HUGE – tri-state fair, drawing people from Arkansas, Tennessee and Mississippi. The rodeo part was scheduled for seven days, with two performances each day. There was also a concert section, with one concert right in the middle of the rodeo so people could have a choice.

Performers included Vince Gill, Chris Ladoux, Doug Superna, and others I can't remember, but they were all big name talents in country music. There were thirteen performances, two a day, with each performer singing twice each day. Later that day, there would be a college football game. Like I said, this place was huge.

We drove around the outside of the place four times and couldn't find the entrance to the rodeo section, and we were beginning to feel panic. Luckily the car I'd rented was a small compact car, so when we passed by a gate where people were lined up to pay to get in the fair, I told Greg Mc to pull up there. The car was small enough to fit inside the opening. When we pulled up to the ticket stand, you should have seen the look on the ticket girl's face. I said, "Do you mind if we open the gate and go through it?"

She was still stunned, so she just nodded her head.

After we got inside the fairgrounds everyone was opening gates for us, even policemen. We didn't know why but we didn't question it – we just took advantage of it. Maybe it was our big cowboy hats or our "down-home" looks. We finally found a parking place but still had to walk a quarter-mile, lugging all of our gear, to the rodeo building.

When we got inside the building Tracy left us to sit in one of the seats designated for contestant's wives or girlfriends and such. Greg Mc and I went to pay our entry fees, which were over $200.

After paying the fees we went behind the bucking chute and got out our stuff: chaps, bull rope, protective vest and spurs, riding boots and riding pants. Then I walked out to the arena. I had ridden in a building before, but this place was different. There was a big screen for re-plays of each ride or buck-off so everyone in the building could watch it again. I was a little intimidated by all of this but I said to myself, "It's just another rodeo."

My bull was all black with no horns, and he weighed

only about 1200 pounds, which is small for a professional bucking bull. A guy named Terry Crowder knew all of the bulls well, and he told me that my bull wasn't very good but Greg Mc had a good one. I told myself that my bull may not be any good but I didn't come all this way and go through all this trouble just to fall off.

Greg Mc was out first, and Terry was right about how good Greg's bull was – he threw Greg Mc off. Then it was my turn. I got down on my bull, Greg Mc pulled my rope, then I slid up and got a good seat. I nodded for the gate to be opened.

When this little bull came out he immediately turned to the left, but it was only a half turn, then he did something very athletic – he reared up like a horse, jumped backwards, and spun to the right, into my riding hand. Ordinarily I would have really spurred him hard, but it was too easy. I was kinda disappointed, so I finished the ride and got off. Truthfully, I was so disappointed I got my bull-rope and went straight out of the arena, not even watching the replay on the big screen.

When they announced my score of 87 I thought someone had added wrong, but when I went to the secretary's office to get my day-money check I looked at the judges' sheets and nobody had added wrong. It really was 87. I turned to Greg Mc and asked, "What did he do that was so great?"

Greg Mc said, "He bucked his butt off and you rode him perfectly."

I couldn't believe it, but suddenly I felt good.

We left the building and started back to our car, but the football game was about to start. We were inside the stadium fence and were trying to get out, but a policeman stopped us and asked for our football tickets. I said, "We're not going to the football game. We were in the rodeo and we're trying to get back to our car."

Would you believe he wouldn't let us go out of there until we showed him our back-numbers and our P.R.C.A. cards. Greg Mc was getting so mad I thought he was going to attack the cop. When we all looked back on it, we laughed. It was kinda funny, stopping us from going out, not in.

We wished we could spend more time in Memphis – maybe seeing the Mississippi River bluffs and Beale Street and Graceland (maybe even Elvis' ghost lurking around) – but we had to get going. We were entered in a rodeo in Marianna, Florida the next day and that was about a 9-hour drive. As we left the outskirts of the city we all said, "Bye bye, Memphis. It was good to know you, even for such a short time."

Daytona, 1994. Pee Wee on Wooley Bully. About 7 seconds into the ride he reached down, pulled the rope's tail and jumped off for absolutely no reason.   Photo: Mike Rastelli

Chapter 23

Back
to
Florida

Tracy, Greg Mc and I took turns driving, and we arrived in Marianna at three in the morning. We got a motel room, and this time there were two beds. Tracy and I slept in one bed, and Greg Mc in the other. Before you jump to conclusions, there was no hanky-panky going on between Tracy and me. We were all exhausted and we fell asleep immediately. And besides that, we would never do such a thing with Greg Mc lying in the next bed.

The rodeo started at three that afternoon. When we got there we were told that only five bullriders had entered and three didn't show, so it was just Greg and me. There was $500 added, and those other guys had to pay their entry fees, so that meant we could win a lot of money. In addition, they had a jackpot bullriding to cover for the lack of P.R.C.A. riders, and they let Greg Mc and me enter that too.

To make a long story short, Greg Mc won first in the P.R.C.A. part and I won second. Greg Mc made about $500 and I won about $400. In the jackpot bullriding I won second but Greg Mc got thrown off. The good part was that the jackpot paid cash, about $125. As always, P.R.C.A. paid with checks. By then we needed the cash.

After the rodeo I treated Tracy and Greg Mc to a big steak dinner in Marianna. I ended up in third place in Memphis and it paid about $1500, and counting Marianna, I won a little over $2000 that weekend. That paid a lot of bills, and I saved some too --for what I can't say yet.

Two weeks later we entered rodeos in Bonifay for Thursday night, Williston for Friday night, and Hollywood (FL) for Saturday night. We couldn't leave for Bonifay until Greg Mc got off work at 5 o'clock, and the rodeo was scheduled to start at eight. Driving at ordinary speed it was about 4-1/2 hours to Bonifay, so we had to drive pretty fast if we even hoped to make it. We were in Janie's car and she was with us.

On the way up we noticed that the car was smoking much more than normal. It smelled like burning oil, but we didn't think much about it. We were running late, and that was the only thing on our minds.

We got to the rodeo arena at about 8:30. Luckily, the P. A. system had gone out, so they hadn't started yet. At big P.R.C.A. rodeos they have two sections of bullriding, one at the beginning and one at the end. Greg Mc and I were in the first section, so we really caught a break when the P. A. system didn't work and delayed the rodeo.

Panama City isn't very far from Bonifay, so my mom met us at the rodeo. She had made me a shirt, so I took off the shirt I was wearing and put on the new one. I think that made her proud. I didn't know it at the time, but later that night I would give her even more reason to be proud of me.

We didn't know any of the bulls because the stock-contractor was from Texas. I asked the flank-man if he could tell me anything about my bull, and he said no, not really. The bull was leased from someone else. I said, "Great."

Greg Mc came out before me and rode his bull, but the bull wasn't very good. He only scored a 72. Then it was my turn. My bull was a big brindle, weighing about 1800 pounds, with short horns about 4 inches long. I asked someone to pull my rope for me, then I slid up, got a good seat, and nodded for the gate.

That bull really blew out of the chute. He took three big jumps then started spinning to the left. It was all I could do to ride him. I had to use all of my strength, finesse and balance, and I got real good holds with my spurs. All of that is important.

When I jumped off the crowd was going crazy, then they announced my score: 88 points! That was the best bullride I had ever made, and I knew it. I threw my hat high in the air.

The bull in Memphis was real easy, but this one wasn't. I'd worked so hard to ride him. There were about six of the top bullriders there, and they all told me, "Great bullride!"

Little ol' me, being congratulated by some of the best bullriders in the world! I was so proud of that, and I know my mom was too.

Chapter 24

The Ride Home

In all the excitement we forgot about all that smoke coming from the car, but we hadn't driven very far from Bonifay when the smoke started getting worse. The car was very low on oil, so we stopped and filled it again. About 50 miles down the road the smoke was really bad.

Greg Mc turned on the inside light and we couldn't even see each other, although we were sitting right next to each other. Poor Janie was in the back seat, so she really had it bad. To other cars on the highway we must have looked like a smoke ball moving along, something right out of a comic movie.

We must have stopped for oil at least ten times. At one store Greg Mc wanted to get something from the trunk. He unloaded everything, including both of our rigging-bags, then he loaded everything back up – well, almost everything. When I backed the car up we heard something going under it – after I had backed all the way over it. We got out to look, and it was Greg Mc's rigging-bag. Nothing was broken, but for months after that he would have an oil stain on his pants where the bag rubbed against his hip when he carried it. The car was covered with oil, especially underneath.

Because of the oil problem, we covered only about 100 miles in 2-1/2 hours. At this rate it would take us forever to get home, if we made it at all. We looked under the hood several times but couldn't find where the oil was coming from.

At the next truck-stop Greg Mc got under the front of the car while I was inside buying more oil. By this time we were buying oil in one-gallon containers, not quarts. Anyway, Greg Mc finally found the problem: there was a hole in the oil filter unit.

I went back inside and asked a waitress if there was an auto parts store anywhere nearby. She said yes, but that it would not open until eight the next morning. It was then 10:30 p.m. We were stuck there for the rest of the night.

This waitress was about twenty-two and pretty cute. She noticed the distress on my face and said, "After I get off in the morning I can take you down there to get what you need, then I'll bring you back here."

I said, "That would be great."

When I told Greg Mc and Janie what the waitress said she would do, they started kidding me about how cute she was and how nice she was being to me. I just laughed with them. I didn't give a hoot about her looks one way or another, but I really did appreciate her offer of help.

After an almost sleepless night sitting in the car, the waitress took me to the auto parts store at 8 a.m. I bought the new filter unit but we didn't have an oil filter wrench to take off the old one and install the new one. I asked the clerk about the cost of a wrench and he said it would be $8. When you're rodeoing you leave home with enough money for gas, food, and minor unforeseen expenses. You can write a check for your entry fees. After we'd bought all that oil I was short on cash, but the waitress knew the manager. She asked him to let me borrow a wrench and she'd bring it right back. He did.

After we changed the filter unit we thanked this nice young lady about a dozen times, then we headed out for home.

Greg Mc was supposed to be at work at 8 a.m., and I was due at my job at 7:30 a.m. We didn't get home until 11:30. We were in a bit of trouble, but both of our bosses were pretty cool about it. When we told the story, they just laughed.

Chapter 25

Success and a Near Miss

Williston, 1994. Pee Wee Mercer in a great ride on bull C33, Skoal's Topgun, that scored 84 points and won him second place. The "bull was spinning left, but he was also 'drifting.' That's why I'm looking over my right shoulder. He's trying to pull me down on his head." Photo: Mike Rastelli

The rodeo that night was in Williston. Since I live 3 miles from the arena – and Greg Mc only 20 miles away – we did manage to get some sleep. The rodeo was scheduled to start at 8 p.m.

The stock-contractor for the rodeo was from Louisiana, and we didn't know anything about the bulls. His name was Vernon Geudry, and he was a very nice person. He said that Greg Mc's two bulls had both been to the N.F.R. and he told Greg Mc what the bulls usually do. This is good to know, but you always ride a bull from jump to jump because they have a mind of their own and can change it at any time – just like any other animal.

Then Vernon told me that both of my bulls had been to the N.F.R., but my second bull had never been ridden successfully. This rodeo was a two-header too (you ride two bulls), but we had to get on both bulls at the end of the rodeo, back to back, meaning that after you get off your first bull you grab your bull-rope and put it on your second bull. That's a lot different from riding a bull at the beginning of the rodeo and one at the end. There's no time for rest between rides.

There were only six bullriders that night and six the next night, so they had to do the same thing. I guess you could say I got lucky. I was the second rider out in the first section and the last in the second section, so I did get at least a little breather. Some of the other guys had to climb directly on their second bull.

My first bull was gray with a white face with big gray spots on it. He had medium-sized horns, about 6-1/2 inches, and was pretty big – about 1800 pounds. I got set on him, then nodded for the gate.

This bull took one jump straight out and then started spinning to the left, doing what is known as drifting. That means while he was spinning he was pushing his body backward with his front legs while his back-end is up. That makes for a very difficult ride. His pushing-back motion wants to pull your upper body down on his head. I kept pushing back with my riding arm and getting good holds with my spurs. There wasn't much finesse involved, just a lot of grit and try.

When the whistle blew I jumped off and started hustling to get my bull-rope so I could hurry back to the chutes. They announced my score: 84 points! I was happy, but I didn't have time to showboat for my hometown crowd. I had another bull to ride. And besides, my hometown crowd was used to seeing me throw my hat high in the air because I'd been doing this since high school rodeo and some of them had watched me since then.

My second bull was the one that had never been ridden. Some of the best riders in the world had been thrown off of him. He was black with a white face, with black spots on it, and his belly was mostly white. He had horns about 8 inches long. He was kinda tall and what we call slab-sided – narrow in his body. He only weighed about 1200 pounds.

Greg Mc pulled my rope for me and I was really excited. I loved getting on bulls that had never been ridden. I slid up, got a good seat, and nodded.

This bull didn't kick when he came out – that gets your upper body leaning back, and that's not good. I reached for the front as hard as I could, and just then he really reared up. His horn hit me under my left arm. In a situation like that the judges won't disqualify you because the bull hit me – I didn't hit the bull. He started spinning to the right. I was riding great, then I don't know what happened. I fell off into my riding hand, and just like that, I was on the ground. I've watched the video again and again, and to this day I don't know how he threw me off.

I jumped up and ran to one of the judges. Both judges have stop watches, and by the watch I was 7.87 seconds. I was that close. That's the longest anyone had ridden him, but it wasn't 8 seconds.

I was so disappointed, but nobody can ride them all, and I was 84 points on one bull. Only one other person, Jason Curry, rode one bull successfully that night, but he was only 65 points.

The next night was Hollywood, about a 3-1/2 hour drive. I drew a bull that I knew, but when he turned back to the left he wasn't like the other two bulls I had been on the last two days. When he turned back, he didn't kick. That makes a bull what is known as "welly," because when they kick they're trying to throw you out of the spin. You can counter this by using your upper body and your free hand, but I hadn't counted on him not kicking. I just fell off inside the well.

Greg Mc won third place but it only paid about $150. I won in Bonifay, and that paid about $1400. I ended up second in Williston, and that paid about $275 – thus I won over $1600 that weekend. This was three weeks before the Circuit Finals. I went to the Finals in 9th place with over $7000 in winnings. Greg Mc didn't make the finals that year.

The Finals were held at the Brighton Seminole Indian Reservation in early November. While attending this rodeo you have three choices: get a motel room in Okeechobee, or one in Lake Placid, or stay in your motor home – but most people don't have motor homes. Like I said once before, Brighton is right out in the middle of the boondocks. It is almost exactly 30 miles from there to either Okeechobee in the east or to Lake Placid in the west. We got motel rooms in Lake Placid. Tracy and my mom and dad were with me. Tracy wasn't comfortable around my parents so I spent the first day listening to her whine about it. Then I just wouldn't listen anymore. I had to concentrate on the rodeo.

We left for the first performance about 6 o'clock. When we got there I went to pay my entry fees and see which bull I'd drawn. I couldn't believe it. I had drawn a bull that hadn't been ridden all year. His name was Mission Impossible.

The man who hauled this bull for my friend, Gene Carter, in Chiefland, was so proud of this little bull. When I came out of the secretary's office I walked up to him and said, "I'm sorry about your luck."

"What do you mean?" he asked, puzzled.

I said, "Mission Impossible is going to be ridden tonight. I've got him."

That was a bit arrogant, I know, but I had been getting on this bull over in Chiefland at Gene's place since the bull was 1-1/2 years old. He bucked me off about as many times as I rode him, but I guess I just had a good feeling that night.

When it was time for the bullriding they told me I'd be the first to go. I hated being first. I think every bullrider hates being first because the judges usually can't score the first ride very high because they don't know how good the other riders may be. In other words, the first ride is how they judge the rest of the rides, kinda like a starting point.

I knew this bull could spin either left or right or both ways. I sat down on him and someone pulled my rope. I slid up, got a good seat, and nodded for the gate. When he turned out he made two jumps out and then started spinning to the right. I rode Mission Impossible for 8 seconds, then I jumped off.

They announced my score as 82 points! I was happy, but I knew my score should have been higher. After the rodeo ended, the judges agreed it should have been higher, but it was too late.

I tied for first with soon-to-be World Champion Bullrider Jerome Davis, who would win the championship the next year. He got the buckle for that go-round. The next two go-rounds weren't very good for me. I got bucked off. Jerome rode his next two bulls and won the 3rd go-round, so he gave me the buckle from the 1st go-round. I said to myself, "What a heck of a nice person and what a nice thing to do!"

Jerome also won the Southeastern Circuit for the most money won in the Circuit.

Chapter 26

Bad
Luck
in
Little
Rock

Two weeks after the Circuit Finals, Greg Mc and I decided to enter a rodeo in Little Rock, Arkansas. Greg Mc was from Monticello, a small town in southern Arkansas. His brother, Mark, still lived there with his family. Our plan was to leave Friday after we got off work. We were entered for Saturday night.

Greg Mc planned the route for us to take, and I have never been on so many highways and roads to go from one place to another, especially during an all-night drive.

I'll give you a brief description. We took Highway 27 North from Williston to Capps; got on I-10 east of Tallahassee; followed I-10 west to Mobile, then on to Gulfport, Mississippi where we took Highway 49 north to Hattiesburg and then on to Jackson. At Jackson, we took I-20 to Vicksburg, crossed the Mississippi River there and continued on to Tallulah, Louisiana. From there we took Highway 65 North, skirting along the west bank of the Mississippi River, through Lake Providence, then into

Arkansas to Eudora; then Highway 8 to Hamburg, and then Highway 81 North to Monticello.

Before we reached Monticello Greg Mc said he would take the "back way" to Mark's house. For the next 10 or 15 miles we were on clay roads. I was so lost I didn't really know if we were in Arkansas or Oklahoma. On top of that, Greg Mc kept messing with me, saying, "Do you know where we are? I hope I can remember where I'm going."

When we finally got to Mark's house, those wet clay roads had turned our rental car from gray to red.

We got there about 9 a.m., and the rodeo didn't start until 8 p.m. that night. Greg Mc introduced me to Mark, Mark's wife Tina, and their two little girls, Megan, age 4, and Nikki, 2-1/2.

After I met everyone I asked if there was some place I could lie down and get some sleep. I had developed a problem that is a big problem for some people who travel a lot: I can't sleep in moving car. I went straight to bed. Greg Mc stayed up for awhile, catching up on family news with Mark and Tina, then he went to sleep too.

Little Rock is an easy 2-1/2 hour drive from Monticello, so Greg and I didn't get up until 4 p.m. After taking showers, we sat down to an early supper. Tina is a great cook. She made fried pork chops, fried chicken, mashed potatoes and gravy, green beans, and corn – all very good.

Seems that almost every time Greg Mc and I go off together something funny happens (sometimes it's not funny 'till later). This time it happened during supper. Greg Mc and I still laugh about it.

We had all just sat down to eat, and Nikki was sitting across the table from me. Before her mama could say that the mashed potatoes were very hot, Nikki put a spoon full in her mouth.

She started screaming and stuck out her tongue. She looked straight at me, and the look on her face was saying, "Hey, you idiot! Help me!"

I couldn't reach across the table, and even if I could have, I wouldn't have known what to do. At that time there was nothing funny about the situation.

Tina was sitting right next to Nikki, and she quickly scraped the potatoes off of Nikki's tongue. I was scared she'd been hurt, but she went right back to eating again. Then I lost it and started laughing really hard. I explained, as best I could, the look on Nikki's face, then everyone started laughing, Nikki too. We must have all laughed for at least five minutes. I still do when I see that look, "Hey, you idiot! Help me!"

Greg Mc, Mark and I left for Little Rock about 5 p.m. It was almost a straight shot from Monticello up to Pine Bluff and then into Little Rock. We got there with time to spare.

The first thing we heard when we reached the rodeo grounds was that someone got shot last night outside the building. That made all of us a little nervous, so we went inside immediately.

I had drawn what seemed to be a good bull. He was red with long horns, but he was pretty small. Greg Mc had drawn a "green" bull. That doesn't mean he was the color green – it means he hadn't been bucking very long. A bull like that can be very dangerous in the chute.

I came out before Greg Mc. Unfortunately, my bull was a little too "sweet" – I relaxed, and he threw me off.

Then it was Greg Mc's turn. His bull was giving him a heck of a time, bucking inside the chute. Greg Mc finally managed to sit down on him, and just when he got his rope set and pulled, the bull came unglued, bucking like crazy still in the chute. He hurt Greg Mc's knee pretty badly. Greg Mc got a shot to nod his head, but his knee was hurting so badly he couldn't ride very far.

After the rodeo we helped Greg Mc to the Justin Sports Medicine trailer so they could look at his knee. Justin team members are real sports doctors and the program is nation-wide, but they can't be at every rodeo. Lucky for us, they were at this one.

While Greg Mc was getting checked out, some of my cousins who live in Little Rock came by to talk with me, but after such a dismal showing by both Greg Mc and myself, the only thing on my mind was getting out of there as soon as possible.

When Greg Mc came out of the trailer, Mark and I helped him to the car, then we got the heck out of there. We didn't even stop to get something to drink until we were 20 miles south of Little Rock. The first think you want after riding is an ice-cold drink, but under the circumstances, we decided we could wait.

We drove back to Mark's house and spent the night, then we left for home the next morning. It was about 1 a.m. Monday when we reached Williston, and we both had to work that day.

We really enjoyed our visit with Mark and Tina and the girls, but our efforts at the rodeo were nothing to crow about. Things like that happen in rodeo, and you have to take the bad times along with the good. There's always another day.

Chapter 27

An Engagement Ring

It is now two weeks before Christmas. The reason I'd saved some of my rodeo winnings was that I went to a jewelry store and bought Tracy an engagement ring. It was a 1/4 carat diamond, small but a real one.

The reason for buying it might not have been exactly the right one, but I did love Tracy. She'd been on my back about getting engaged, so I felt kinda pressured. We'd been dating for over a year, which was longer than I had dated Jennifer or Molly.

I picked up Tracy at her house, and it was now two days before Christmas. I had the ring in my pocket, waiting for the right moment to give it to her.

During the entire trip into town, Tracy complained about not being engaged. We went to a Wal-Mart for her to do some last minute shopping. I got out of the truck, tossed the ring to her and said, "Here, we're engaged now."

Not very romantic I know, but I had heard enough. I told her we would not get married until she finished college. That degree was very important to her, and since it was important to her, it was also important to me. She wanted to be an agricultural teacher. No degree, no teaching career.

This was December 1994, and she wasn't supposed to graduate until sometime in '96. The way things turned out, it's good for both of us we waited.

Ocala, FL., 1995. "Time for Freedom Bullriding," Pee Wee riding David Carter bull #22, Top Cat, for a score of 74. "Second bull at this two-header, I won third in the average." Photo: Mike Rastelli

Chapter 28

1995 – Pensacola First

There were two rodeos the first weekend in January, and because of some family business, Greg Mc couldn't go to the first one. A friend of mine from Chiefland, Billy, had just gotten his P.R.C.A. permit, so we decided to go to a rodeo in Pensacola.

My mom was still in Panama City, so we went up a day early and spent the night with her and Grandpa. The rodeo started the next day, Friday at 8 p.m. Pensacola is only about 100 miles from Panama City, so we didn't leave for the rodeo until 4 p.m.

Mom went with us. We went in her car because my little Mitsubishi pickup truck would have been too cramped for the three of us. Mom took Highway 98, the road that runs right along the coast, and we saw some really pretty beaches. Traffic was heavy but we still got there right at 8. p.m.

We knew most of the stock-contractor's bulls, but

wouldn't you know it, I drew a bull I didn't know. He was a big black bull, about 1800 pounds, with one short horn.

I got on him, someone pulled my rope, then I slid up and nodded. He blew out of the chute and immediately started spinning to the left. This bull was tricky. When he made the first three rounds he was kicking, which was trying to throw me out of the spin; then he stopped kicking, which was trying to bring me down inside the spin. I recovered from that – I mean I got out of the well – then he started kicking again. I had to fight to get back inside a little bit so he couldn't throw me outside.

Finally the whistle blew, and the rascal just stopped. You never, never get off of a bull that has stopped. If you do, while you are jumping off he can turn on you before you have a chance to do anything.

The bullfighters got the bull to move, but when he did, he ran forward a little. I had already undone my wrap. He ran me back on his butt and then kicked up, which sent me flying straight up about 10 feet into the air. I landed flat on my back. This would have knocked the breath out of me, but as always, I was wearing my protective vest. I got my bull-rope and headed out of the arena, then they announced my score: 84 points! I threw my hat high in the air, like I usually do when I think I've made a good ride.

I didn't start wearing a protective vest until early '94, but they weren't available until late '93. They are very important in protecting your ribs and vital organs. You might think that being hooked by a bull is the most dangerous part of riding bulls, but remember, that bull can weigh anywhere from 1000 to over 2000 pounds. Being stepped on can cause serious injury or could be fatal. If vests had been around for a long time, a lot of cowboy's lives would have been saved, and a lot of injuries would have been prevented. Unfortunately, as I was to learn, they can't protect your whole body.

Billy's turn came up and he was thrown off, so we

left soon after this. Since this was a two-day rodeo I couldn't find out until later how well I had done and how much money I would receive. I would have to call back Monday and the check would be mailed to me.

We stopped in Panama City and again spent the night with Mom, and then we drove on home the next day.

The next night I was entered in a rodeo in Clewiston. Well, it wasn't exactly in Clewiston – it was on the Big Cypress Seminole Indian Reservation 30 miles south of Clewiston. Four of us went together in a rental car: Greg Mc, Billy, a guy named John and myself. None of us liked John, but nobody should have to travel alone, so we decided to take him with us.

When we reached Clewiston we were running late. The rodeo started at 8 p.m. and it was already 7:15. The road to the reservation arena is called "Snake Road," and for a good reason. It curves back and forth like a snake on hot sand. Driving fast is impossible. We got there a little past 8 p.m., but we were okay.

Greg Mc and I were in the first section and they had just finished the Grand Entry. We had to hurry and pay our fees, then get our equipment ready.

I drew a white bull. He was short and fat and he didn't have horns. He didn't do much, just jumped and kicked in a wide circle. I rode him but didn't score many points, something like 64. Greg Mc and John rode their bulls too, but Billy got thrown off. None of us placed, but at least three of us got some day-money. That's better than nothing.

After I'd ridden I was standing behind the bucking chute watching the other riders when a guy named Jason Curry came up to me. He was winning the bullriding at that time. We made small talk for a few minutes, then Jason said, "Why don't you and I go to some rodeos together? I like the way you ride."

I said, "Well, I'm kinda short on travel money, but I think I did pretty good in Pensacola Friday night. We left early so I'm not sure. Let me find out how I did up there and I'll call you Monday."

I found out Monday I'd won the bullriding in Pensacola and it paid $875. I called Jason that night and said, "I did great, so let's enter some rodeos together. I'm ready when you are."

Dade City, FL., 1995. Pee Wee riding a "green bull" belonging to Rusty Willis. "He bucked real good for about six seconds then stopped, so I got a re-ride." (See the next page for a shot of the re-ride). Photo: Mike Rastelli

Chapter 29

Cajun Country and a Fast Ride Home

Dade City, FL., 1995. Pee Wee's re-ride bull, Sky Hook, belonged to 5 Star and "he threw me off." Photo: Mike Rastelli

The first rodeo Jason and I entered together was in Lake Charles, Louisiana, on I-10 about 30 miles from the Texas border, almost a 14-hour drive from my house. Jason lived in Clewiston, about 3-1/2 hours from me, and he got here that Friday about 5 p.m.

We were going in a rental car, which I had already brought over from Ocala. As soon as Jason got here he loaded his rigging-bag and a change of clothes, and we took off.

We'd gotten a few miles down the road when Jason said, "Oh, by the way, we're entered in a rodeo Sunday afternoon at 3 p.m. in Ft. Myers."

Ft. Myers is about a 5-hour drive south from my house. I couldn't believe what I'd heard. I said, "You did what? There's no way we can drive from Lake Charles Saturday night and be in Ft. Myers by 3 p.m. Sunday!"

"Sure we can," he said nonchalantly, as if we had rented a helicopter.

I thought this guy must be crazy, and I wondered what I'd gotten myself into.

We drove all night, stopping only for gas, and it was 6 a.m. when we reached Lake Charles. Both of us were in need of at least a few hours of sleep. For some reason the motels were full. We drove around and around the city, checking each one until we finally found one with an empty room – but we soon found out it was in a bad part of town. The motel was also home to a bunch of crack dealers and prostitutes, and the action was going on even that early. Jason fell on a bed and tuned out immediately, but I couldn't sleep. I stayed awake watching my rental car, making sure nobody stole it.

Jason got up about 11 a.m., then we took showers and went to find a place to eat. I don't recall the name of the restaurant, but it was definitely in the better part of town. We walked in wearing our Wranglers, boots, pull-over shirts, belts and buckles, and our cowboy hats. Everyone else was dressed in business suits. Jason and I looked at each other and said, "What the hell," then we walked in and sat down.

When the waitress brought us the menus we looked at the prices and knew why everyone was dressed up. We were hungry, so decided to stay anyway. There was stuff on the menu that looked inviting, like red beans and rice with Cajun sausage, Crawfish Etouffee, Cajun Jambalaya, seafood gumbo, and a Muffuletta sandwich. We didn't know how any of that would set on a stomach jarred by a bucking bull so we went for something simple – country fried steak and mashed potatoes.

I don't know why this place was so popular, but it was jammed full. After we ordered it took 45 minutes to get our food, and our orders were simple. By the time we finished eating and paid the bill it was 3 p.m.

The rodeo didn't start until 8 p.m., but we still had to find the coliseum where the rodeo was being held. We drove around for a long time looking for it without success, then we stopped and asked someone for directions. It's no wonder we couldn't find it – it was at least 5 miles out of town.

We reached the coliseum at 5:30 and decided to go on in and relax. At most indoor rodeos they have a hospitality room for contestants and everyone else involved with the rodeo, such as judges and the stock-contractor and his crew. There are lots of places to sit and also food, cold drinks, beer, and bottled water. They're really nice.

This one in Lake Charles was especially nice. I sat down in a comfortable leather chair and fell asleep. I hadn't slept since we left Florida. As I said, I can't sleep anymore in a moving car, and I didn't sleep at the motel because I was worried about the rental car.

Jason shook me awake at 7:30, then we headed back behind the bucking chutes to start getting ready. We were in the first section, so that would give us a little more time to get back home.

As I have said previously, I live only about 25 miles from Gainesville, and when the University of Florida Gators play a home football game, I swear you can hear the roar all the way to my house. Well, that's nothing compared to what these Louisiana folks do at a rodeo. They really have a good time. I've never heard such whoopin' and hollerin', even before the first bull is let loose.

That sort of crowd reaction usually pumps up the adrenaline and you do your very best, but this time it had a reverse reaction. I don't know if I was rattled or if it was just a lack of sleep, but I got bucked off very quickly. It didn't seem to matter to the crowd – they cheered me anyway, just as if I had scored a 99. I almost threw my hat high in the air.

Jason's bull didn't buck good enough, so he got a re-ride. That didn't last long either. As soon as he was out of the arena we put all of our gear back in our bags and loaded them in the car for that long drive home.

Jason's re-ride set us back time-wise, and we didn't get out of the parking lot until 10 p.m. We had 17 hours to make the trip from Lake Charles to Ft. Myers, but we still had to stop at my house, drop off the rental car, get Jason's truck, and go on to Ft. Myers.

After we got back on I-10 East we really put the pedal to the metal, but the faster we drove, the more time it seemed we were losing. As you know, the world spins from east to west, and it seemed as though the world was turning against us – literally.

We finally arrived at my house at 10:30 a.m., then we loaded our gear into Jason's truck. I told Dad he would have to take the rental car back to Ocala for me.

We left for Ft. Myers immediately. The bullriding started at 3 p.m., so we had a little over 4 hours to make a normal 5-hour drive. Tracy was to meet me at the rodeo and bring me home. She had just bought a new car, a little Mazda, so she didn't mind.

Jason drove really fast. We got there at 2:30, a full half-hour before the rodeo started. I couldn't believe we actually made it.

The bullriding was a two-header, so it paid each go-round and an average. I won the first go-round and had the bull to win the second go-round and the average, but I got bucked off. Jason got bucked off the first go-round and won the second go-round. We both made over $300.

Just as soon as I finished, Tracy and I headed home. All I wanted to do at that point was sleep. Travel-wise, it had been a most unusual weekend.

Chapter 30

Jason Does It Again

Immokalee, FL., 1995. Pee Wee, riding bull #75, Fire, placed 4th with a score of 75. Same ride as cover shot. Photo: Mike Rastelli

During the ride home from Ft. Myers I remember saying to Tracy, "I hope Jason never does anything like this again." But, he did. He got me a couple more times.

The next month, the first weekend in February, Jason entered us in a rodeo in Jackson, Mississippi. This was great, because the Jackson rodeo is a big one with lots of money to be won. He entered us for Friday. But the problem was, he entered us in two Florida rodeos for the next two days, Saturday afternoon in Homestead and Sunday afternoon in Immokalee. When he told me this I said, "Are you crazy? Jackson is a 15-hour drive from here, and Homestead is a 6-1/2-hour drive south of my house."

He said again, without concern, "We can make it."

We left for Jackson Thursday afternoon. I started off driving when Jason had a great idea – he'd get some Vivarin to make him stay awake and help drive. Yeah, it was a great idea. Vivarin is loaded with caffeine. All it did was make Jason sick to his stomach, and I drove 15 hours straight by myself.

Jason finally went to sleep, and I woke him up when I pulled into a motel on the outskirts of Jackson. It was 6:30 a.m. We got a room and slept for a few hours. We both got up at noon, took showers, then went to a Burger King to eat. After having our "nutritious" meals – that's about as nutritious as a rodeo cowboy usually gets – we headed into Jackson to find the coliseum where the rodeo was to be held.

The rodeo started at 3 p.m., but remember, that's Central time. We were in the first round of riders. While waiting our turns, I noticed that these Mississippi folks really enjoyed rodeo, like those audiences in Louisiana. And I'll tell you something else: they have some pretty "cowgirls" up there in Mississippi, the kind that make your eyeballs pop out of the sockets.

I rode my bull but he wasn't very good, so I only got some day-money. Jason got bucked off. It wasn't exactly what you would call a financial success, but we enjoyed it. When the crowd is in high spirits, the riders are in high spirits, win or lose.

When I was waiting to get my day-money check a man of about fifty came up to me and said, "You Florida boys like good vittles?"

I said, "Sure."

He told me on our way home tomorrow to stop down Highway 49 in Mendenhall and eat at noon at the Mendenhall Hotel revolving tables. He said they pile the second level of the table with every home-cooked food you can imagine, then you just turn the table around and around and help yourself to all you can eat of everything. I thanked him for the information although I knew we would never see the Mendenhall Hotel. As I said before, you miss a lot of things when you are on the fast-track rodeo circuit.

We left Jackson at 6 p.m. and drove as fast as we could, but when we hit the Florida State Line, winds were blowing at 35 mph and gusting up to 55 mph That slowed us down because it was hard just to keep the car on the road.

We drove all night and got back to my house about 10:30 a.m. The rodeo in Homestead started at 2 p.m., so there was no way we could make that drive in a little over 3 hours. We would have to cancel out in Homestead, but Jason insisted on trying one more thing. He called his girlfriend, Shell, in Clewiston and explained the situation. She said she would see what she could do. About 30 minutes later, she called back and said there is a commuter flight from Gainesville to Miami at noon, and the tickets are $99 each. She would meet us at the Miami airport and take us on from there. We decided to try it.

I have enjoyed some flights before, but this time I was hesitant. The wind was still bad, and besides that, the bull I'd drawn in Homestead wasn't very good. Jason really wanted to do this, so I finally said, "O.K."

Tracy drove us to the airport in Gainesville, then we bought our tickets hurriedly and boarded the plane. The take-off was very, very shaky. The wind threw that small plane around like a tin can. I was scared. I said to Jason, "We're going to die!"

We had been tossed around for about twenty minutes when it finally calmed down. I asked the flight attendant what happened, and she said we were temporarily above the bad winds. In another half-hour we were circling the Miami Airport. The wind was just as bad there, so the landing wasn't any less scary than the take-off.

That plane ride put goosebumps on me, but I didn't know how scared I was about to be. Shell and Jason's mom met us at the airport, and we quickly got to Shell's car and loaded up. By then it was almost 1 p.m.

Homestead is about an hours' drive from Miami, but

the traffic going down there was almost bumper to bumper. Shell drove like a maniac, passing cars in the turn lane, weaving in and out of traffic, sometimes whipping in front of cars and missing their front bumpers by inches, going 50 or 60 mph in 35 mph zones. Several times I thought I would soil my jeans, and I said silently, "Never again."

We got to the arena in Homestead about ten minutes till 2 p.m. I couldn't believe it. The little fart had been right again.

I called Jason "little fart" because he is only 5'3" tall. Shell is the same height, so they make a perfect pair.

Anyway, Jason's bull was pretty good, and he won first. My bull was better than I had expected, and I won third. Jason won a little over $400, and I won $200.

After the rodeo we went to Jason's parent's home, just outside of Clewiston. I don't know what time it was when we got there, but I was totally exhausted. I just wanted some sleep. They put me on the couch, and I was asleep before my head hit the pillow. I slept so hard, the next morning I woke up with a kinda hang-over.

After we had all eaten breakfast we got ready to go to Immokalee, which is only about an hour and a half drive. The rodeo there is on a Seminole Indian Reservation, but it's not as desolate as some of them. Immokalee is a small town and the arena is just outside of town.

I drew a pretty good bull and he was really fun to ride. I won third, and Jason didn't place, but he did get a little day-money.

On the way back home, I still couldn't believe we'd been to rodeos in Jackson, Homestead, and Immokalee in only three days time. What a trip that was!

The next weekend we entered the Silver Spurs Rodeo, which is a big event in Kissimmee. The "Crackers" really come out for this one, especially since Osceola County was once the heart of pioneer cattle country. Kissimmee, the county seat, was called Cow Town back then. Even today, most of the land from Kissimmee south down through Kenansville and Yeehaw Junction and Fort Drum to Okeechobee is still cattle country.

Neither one of us did very well – we both got bucked off. When you go to Silver Spurs you expect the bulls to buck really hard, and you've got to be at the top of your form. I guess we had a let down after all that travel, but that's rodeo.

Kissimmee, FL., July 4,1995. Pee Wee riding Silver Spurs Rodeo bull #35, Big Red, for a score of 74 and a 4th place finish. This was his "re-ride bull." "Standing on the back of my chute [4] is Greg Mc in the black hat and Jason Curry in the sunglasses and straw hat. Greg pulled my rope and Jason 'spotted' me. Photo: Mike Rastelli

Chapter 31

Georgia & Alabama and a Wild Night in the Woods

Okeechobee, March, 1995. Pee Wee on Silver Spur's bull #19, Buck Island Express. The 74 points he got for this ride won him 3rd place. Photo: Mike Rastelli

A week later we were entered in a rodeo in Perry, Georgia for Friday night and Birmingham, Alabama for Sunday. Jason's dad went with us.

Perry is on I-75 south of Macon. Once you get on I-75 at Ocala or Gainesville it's just a straight shot up there. The rodeo didn't start until 8 p.m., so we took our time going.

We were cruising along I-75 when all of a sudden Jason started yelling at his dad, "Pull in! Pull in!"

I was startled and didn't know what was going on, but Jason's dad just smiled and pointed to a Krystal hamburger joint sign. He explained to me that Jason is addicted to those little square hamburgers. They're just like White Castle up north. I like both of them, but they're not worth all that fuss. After Jason ate his fill we headed north again.

The event in Perry is a big fair, livestock show, and rodeo. My cousin Greg Mercer, his wife Connie, and their new baby girl, Madison, were supposed to be there.

We reached the fairgrounds at 5:30 p.m. I walked around the livestock exhibits looking for Greg and his family but didn't see them.

About 7 p.m. Jason and I went behind the bucking chutes to get ready. I was strapping on my spurs when Greg came up behind me and said, "Hey, are you a Mercer?"

I looked up, grinned and said, "Hey, man! What you been up to?"

We talked for a few minutes, and he told me where they were sitting. After I got everything ready I went up into the stands to meet Connie and see the baby, but the visit didn't last long. I was in the first section, so I had to go.

The bull I had wasn't that great. I only got some day-money, and Jason got bucked off. As soon as we said goodbye to Greg and Connie we loaded up the car and headed to Birmingham.

Although we didn't have to, we drove most of the night. Mr. Curry wanted to go on to Birmingham non-stop. We reached the city at 2 a.m. and drove around looking for a motel with a vacancy. The only one we could find was a Hampton Inn with rooms priced at $125 a night. We weren't too crazy about that but we were tired, so we checked in.

We weren't up until Sunday so we spent Saturday driving around and seeing the sights. We went to the rodeo Saturday night just to watch. Sitting in the stands with nothing to do was a rare treat. We relaxed and cheered the riders.

The rodeo started the next day at 2 p.m. Jason and I both rode our bulls, but they weren't very good. We only got some day-money, but we all had lots of fun on that little trip.

The next month, March, Jason and I entered rodeos at Arcadia on Friday and Okeechobee on Saturday. Both rodeos started at 2 p.m.

I rode down to Arcadia Thursday afternoon with Rusty Willis. The stock-contractor had leased some of Rusty's bulls and he was taking them down for the rodeo. Tracy was to meet me there the next day. After unloading the bulls Rusty and I went to get motel rooms for the night.

At the rodeo the next day I drew one of Rusty's bulls but he fouled me at the chute gate. You're supposed to get a re-ride when that happens, but the judges wouldn't give me a re-ride. Rodeo is like any other sport: one day the call may go against you even though it's very wrong, and the next day the call may be in your favor. You have to take it both ways.

Jason rode his bull and got some day-money, then it was time to move on. As I got into the car with Tracy, Jason leaned out his truck window and said, "Ya'll follow me."

We were going to Clewiston to meet up with Shell and then go to her sister's place where we would spend the night. When we got there Shell introduced us to her sister, Charity, and her husband. They were leaving to go somewhere.

After we all freshened up we went to Clewiston to have supper at Sonny's Barbecue, which must be a popular place because we had to wait a half-hour to get a table. After piling up a mound of rib bones we left and went back to the trailer. It was a three-bedroom trailer but there were no beds in two of the bedrooms. Shell and Jason had stayed there before, and all they had was a mattress on the floor in their room. Tracy and I had to sleep on the bare floor that night.

After breakfast the next morning we went on to Okeechobee for the rodeo there. I had a pretty good bull, but Jason had a really good bull. I rode my bull and scored 73 points, which placed me second at that time. Jason got thrown off.

As soon as our rides were over we left immediately. I didn't even pick up my day-money check. Jason's brother, Buddy, was up the next day so I asked him to pick it up for me.

We were in a hurry because it was Shell's birthday and her mother was throwing a party for her. When we got there, Tracy and I were introduced to Shell's mom and dad, and they were very nice people. By the way, Shell isn't short for Michelle. I found that out the hard way. I called her Michelle and she said quickly, "My name isn't Michelle! It's Rosshelle!"

I was so surprised I just said, "Yes Ma'am." Even though Shell is 4 or 5 years younger than me I had been set straight, and I knew it.

A friend of Jason and Shell – I think his name was Tim – was at the party, and he invited several of us out to this place where he was the caretaker/hunting guide for a group of lawyers from Miami.

When we got there we went to Tim's trailer. He had two 4-wheelers parked beside the trailer. Then he took us on through the woods to what those lawyers called a "hunting camp." There were six more 3-wheelers and 4-wheelers parked there.

We took a tour of the lodge, and it was something else. They had a hot tub, too many bedrooms to count, three bathrooms with a bidet in each of them (first bidet I'd ever seen — I asked Tim what they were, and when he explained it, I fell out laughing), a big stone fireplace in the main room and also central heat and air.

This place wasn't a "hunting camp" – it was a

sanctuary, just a place to get away from wives and jobs for a few days at a time. It was really a joke. Maybe they did occasionally kill a wild hog or a deer, but that wasn't the main purpose.

We went back outside and got on those little "swamp buggers." I picked a 3-wheeler and Tracy got on behind me. Jason and Shell got on a 4-wheeler, and off we all roared into the darkness. We were slinging mud and having a lot of fun.

We finally stopped and traded places. Tracy got on with Shell, and Jason got on with me. We did this so Jason and I could do some crazy stunts we couldn't do with the girls. We must have wrecked a half dozen times, but we were having a blast. It was almost as much fun as riding a bucking bull.

All of a sudden we broke out of the woods and entered the prairie. The moon had come up, bathing everything with a dim glow, and we could see little hammocks scattered everywhere. As we raced across the land, streaming moonlight behind us like a jet stream, we must have looked like a couple of banshees, wailing and riding a broomstick. If anyone could have seen us it would have scared the hell out of them.

After circling several hammocks we turned back. Most people would have been hopelessly lost out there, but I had been on prairies all my life, day and night, and I sensed the right way to return.

When we entered the woods it became dark again. We went back by where we left the girls and noticed they seemed to be stuck in mud, so we drove out to help them. As we got off our 3-wheeler and walked to them they suddenly bombarded us with mud, then they took off laughing.

I know we all had lots and lots of fun that night. Little did I know this would be the last wild, carefree romp-in-the-woods I would have in my lifetime. Unknown to me, the doomsday clock was ticking.

Later that night we all went back to Charity's place, took showers, and went to bed. The next morning, after breakfast, Tracy and I thanked Jason and Shell, said our good-byes, and headed home.

On the way back all Tracy and I could talk about was the night before, and how much fun we had. Oh, I did stop and get my check from Buddy. I ended up in 3rd place, and with my day-money, I won over $300.

Arcadia, FL., March, 1995. Pee Wee, riding a green bull belonging to Rusty Willis. This was the only time he ever saw this bull and couldn't remember its number. "I got fouled at the gate, got off and 'declared myself,' but the judges wouldn't give me a re-ride." Photo: Mike Rastelli

Chapter 32

**A Check
Snafu
and a
Painful
Injury**

There were no rodeos the next weekend. When I wasn't on the road to a rodeo I tried to spend the weekend with Tracy, but it didn't always work out that way. Sometimes I'd go to a bar with my friend, Joe. Tracy still wasn't twenty-one, so she couldn't be served alcohol, and it did get kinda boring just sitting there – so she wouldn't go. We didn't go to a bar to pick up women – well, at least I didn't – it was just to have a few beers and relax. Sometimes Tracy would get mad about this, and other times she wouldn't.

The next weekend Jason and I entered rodeos in Lake City for Friday night and Montgomery, Alabama for Saturday afternoon. This was the first time Shell went with us, and we were driving a rental car.

When we got to Lake City it was pouring rain. We stopped at a convenience store and asked the clerk where the rodeo was being held. He told us to go down this road beside the store and we would see it on the left.

The traffic on the main highway in front of the store was really heavy and moving slow because of the rain, so we decided to drive behind the store to get to the road. Jason was driving. On this little dirt road up ahead there seemed to be a big mud puddle, but when we hit it, it was very deep. The front of the car sank down, and water came almost over the hood. We all said in unison, "Oh, no!"

But we made it through. When we reached the rodeo grounds everything was mud. The parking lot was a muddy field, and the arena was a sea of mud. Now, cowboys since rodeo got its start back in the 10s or 20s have dealt with these conditions and a lot worse, and so have Jason and I. It's no fun, but rodeos aren't like baseball – they're not called on account of rain or mud or much of anything else. The show goes on, regardless.

Jason and I found a dry place under the tongue of a goose-neck trailer to get out our equipment and keep our ropes dry. That's important because we use rosin, which is nothing but dried pine tar on the hand hold of the bull rope and the tail of the rope. We don't rosin the whole tail, just the part that's going into your hand. Pitchers in baseball use rosin to get a better grip on the baseball, but they use the powder of the rosin. We use the rocks of rosin. I know I haven't mentioned this before, and it's such an important part of our equipment. So, I guess, you've just learned something else about rodeo.

I had a pretty good bull. I'd never been on him but I'd watched him at several rodeos, and I liked him. He was a black bull with horns, but the horns were cut back and really big at the ends. Every time I'd watched this bull he'd buck straight out from the chute one or two jumps and then spin to the right, which was great. Well, this time he must have been scared to get his feet wet. When he came out he bucked around until he found a dry spot, then he spun to the right. By then my rope was wet, and my hand slipped down to the bottom of the hand hold. That loosened my rope, but fortunately the whistle blew and I got off.

As soon as my feet touched the ground that bull hit me hard in my chest with his horn, knocking me back about 10 feet, flat on my back. If it hadn't been for my protective vest it would have broken my sternum for sure, but I just got up and walked away.

Jason rode his bull too, but it was kinda comical. His bull ran straight across the arena, just jumping over mud puddles, then he turned right and ran down along the fence, doing the same thing – jumping over mud puddles. Everyone was laughing. When the whistle blew, Jason jumped off and landed face first into a big puddle. This brought the house down, and everyone really laughed and cheered.

After we'd collected our winnings and put our gear away, we got back in the car. We were both soaked and cold, but after a few minutes with the heater on, we felt better. We stopped down the road and put on some dry clothes, then we headed to Montgomery.

We drove straight through and got there about 2:30 a.m., then we drove around looking for a place to stay. We finally found a motel with a vacancy, not a chain one like Holiday Inn or such, just a nice little local motel.

We all slept good and didn't get up until 10 a.m. We were in no hurry because the rodeo didn't start until 3 p.m. After showers we got dressed and went out to eat at a nearby Shoney's, then we went to the Coliseum where the rodeo was to be held. It was only 1:30 or so, but we decided to go in and relax in the hospitality room. At 2:30 Jason and I went behind the chutes to get ready.

We were in the first section, so they loaded our bulls first. I didn't know the bull I'd drawn, and there was a good reason: he was a "green bull." He was really, really bad in the chute. Every time I tried to get set he'd start bucking, and I couldn't sit on him. The stock-contractor finally came up and said, "Hurry up, boy!"

I said, "If he'll give me half a shot I'll call for him."

I'd already tried three times to get out on him, and there's a rule that states that after three tries you can ask the judges for a re-ride; but this little bull had pissed me off and I was determined to get on him. He finally settled down long enough for me slide up to my rope, so I nodded for the gate.

He bucked straight out from the chute, then he made a circle right back to the chute. He jumped sideways into the chute, smashing my right leg between him and the metal chute. I tried to jerk my leg up, but my foot still got smashed. Despite the contact with my whole foot, my heel was the only thing that really hurt.

The stock-contractor came back behind the chute where I was sitting down and in quite a bit of pain. He said, "Son, you've got a re-ride if you want it."

I said, "Yes, sir, but could I take it tonight instead of right now?"

He said, "No problem."

I knew I'd gotten his respect by what's known as "cowboying up" and getting out on the bull even though I didn't have to.

Jason got bucked off, but we had to stay until the night performance starting at 8 p.m. We went back to the motel to relax, and I iced down my heel really good.

We went back to the rodeo for my re-ride, but my heel hurt so badly I couldn't get a hold with my spur on the right side. My bull spun to the right, and I just couldn't ride without being able to get a hold with that foot. It didn't last long – I hit the deck in no time flat. We waited for that re-ride for nothing. I was disappointed, but Jason and Shell didn't worry about it at all.

Good thing we didn't have another rodeo to make. The next month, April, and most of May, I laid off because of my heel.

The last weekend in May Jason and I entered a rodeo in Athens, Georgia. I had a good bull and rode him. I placed 3rd and it paid over $500. Jason rode his bull but only got some day-money.

There was a problem with my check that I didn't notice until I tried to cash it. The rodeo secretary forgot to sign it. But I thought, "No problem."

We'd entered Asheville, North Carolina for the next weekend, the first weekend in June. I figured the same secretary would be there, but, boy, was I wrong! I left the house with only $50 in my pocket and a check for over $500. I thought I'd just get her to cash it for me.

I went up there with Jason and an old high school rodeo buddy of mine, Doug. We went in Doug's big conversion van, and the only problem was that it didn't get very good gas mileage. It cost $30 just to fill it once.

By the time I'd bought my tank of gas and eaten I had $5 when we got to Asheville; but I still thought, "No problem."

When we got to the rodeo about 6:30 p.m. I found there was a very big problem. The rodeo secretary wasn't the same one that gave me the check. I didn't have any money for my entry-fees, not to mention I didn't have any money to get home on. Jason and Doug would let me slide on my part of the expenses, because that's how rodeo cowboys are, but I still didn't have my entry-fees, and I didn't have enough money in the bank to write a check. I'd written hot checks before and I always won enough money to beat them back to the bank, but I had a feeling that might not be the case this time. Luckily for me, the stock-contractor was Leroy Mason. He paid my entry-fees and cashed a check for $50 so I could get back home.

I was right not to write a check for my entry-fees. I got bucked off, so I wouldn't have had the money to beat the check back to the bank. The P.R.C.A. will let card holders write a check for their entry-fees, but if you bounce three checks you're not allowed to write another one to the P.R.C.A. I'd already bounced one check. It was just a mix-up at my bank, but I still had one strike against me. Jason and Doug got bucked off too, but they didn't go off to North Carolina with just $50 in their pockets.

I finally got that secretary to cash the check for me a week later. The rest of June I didn't go to any rodeos, so I spent time with Tracy and my job at the door-mill.

I saw Tracy as much as I could. I'd take her out to supper when I had the money. Even though I'd won a little rodeo money here and there, most of it went to bills, but I treated her as good as I could.

When Tracy was living in a dorm room at the University her mother gave her only $20 per week to live on. I'd go see her at least twice a week and take her out to eat. I'd always give her the money and ask her to pay the bill, but if the check was $10, I'd give her $15, like I didn't know how much it was, and tell her to keep the change. I always gave her $5 more than the check.

I know $10 a week isn't much, but that's all I could do at that time. If I could give more, I would – and did.

Tracy eventually moved back in with her parents, but the commute from there to Gainesville was too far. From her house to Gainesville was 45 miles, which meant 90 miles per day. From my house it's only about 25 miles to Gainesville. To save so much commuting time, she moved in with my parents and me.

In July I'd planned on just two rodeos, one in Tunica, Mississippi and one in Marianna. Jason and I would go to Tunica together, and Greg Mc and I to Marianna. Tunica was scheduled for the first weekend, and Marianna the next.

One day Jason called me and said, "Hey man, why don't we go to the rodeo in Cheyenne?"

My first reaction was to say, "Great, let's go."

After I hung up the phone I realized I didn't have the money to go to Cheyenne, but there was a chance. The Tunica rodeo would be the largest paying rodeo in the southeast, with $10,000 added. There was also Marianna, but it was only $500 added, and that wasn't enough – so I thought. But if I could do good at Tunica I could afford to go to Wyoming.

After Jason entered us in Tunica he called me and said, "I've entered us in a rodeo in Auxvasse, Missouri just before Tunica."

I was dumbfounded. I finally said, "You did what? Don't you ever look at a map before you enter us in a rodeo? Do you know how far it is from here to Missouri and then back to Mississippi? We'll have to cross parts of several states just to get up there."

I was really mad. I was counting on a nice easy ride up to Mississippi, and this meant we'd have to leave two days earlier than I'd planned. I finally calmed down and said to myself, "Oh well, it's not that big of a deal."

But I didn't know what we were in for.

Chapter 33

Auxvasse
& Tunica
& More

The first thing I did was get out my atlas and see if I could find Auxvasse on the Missouri map. When I finally found it my eyes just about jumped out of my head – it's only about 100 miles east of Kansas City, on Highway 54 six miles north of Interstate 70. It is also 10 miles south of Mexico, Missouri.

I had to ask Greg Mc how to pronounce Auxvasse, and somehow he knew. It sounds like you are saying "aw" and then "vase" like a rich person says it. Now you know.

I always picked the route for our out-of-state trips, and I sorta picked the scenic route rather than the most direct route. I guess I was just tired of nothing but interstate highways.

The next Thursday, Jason and Shell picked me up at my house about 5:30 p.m. and we headed out. We drove north through Georgia, through a small part of western North Carolina and eastern Tennessee, into Kentucky, and then to St. Louis, the Gateway to the West.

Jason and I drove all night to get there. As soon as we entered St. Louis he woke Shell up, and the clicking started.

Shell is a camera nut. She's always taking pictures, and she's pretty good at it. I think she snapped a picture of everything in the city as we passed through it.

From there we headed west on Interstate 70 until we found the Highway 54 exit, then we got off and turned north. It was about 4:20 p.m. when we reached the exit, and we checked into our motel rooms a few minutes later. Shell had reserved the rooms in advance since there is only one motel in the area.

Auxvasse is literally a dot on the map, and if you blink, you'll miss it. There is a truck stop, a truck wash, a local restaurant, the one motel, and that's about it. According to my atlas, the population is 812. Probably a good quiet place to live and raise kids.

The rodeo didn't start until 8 p.m., and it was only 5 miles away, so we did get a little rest. We finally left the motel and headed north again.

It must have rained there too, because it was muddy – but this wasn't normal mud. This stuff stuck to everything you were wearing and your equipment, even if you just got close to it. It even stuck to itself.

Well, to make a long story short, I rode my bull but only got a little day-money. For some reason I can't explain, I didn't get much mud on my equipment or myself. On the other hand, Jason got bucked off, and almost everything about him and his gear was muddy and kinda damp.

We didn't do so hot in the rodeo, but those folks there really appreciated two little "Florida Crackers" coming all the way up there to participate in their local rodeo. They cheered and shook our hands, and we all walked out of there about 6 inches taller.

We left the rodeo grounds and stopped at the truck wash to clean the mud off our equipment, and we got another surprise. The force of the water in the main faucet was so great that if you put your head in front of it, it would cut your skin or give you a crew-cut. It blew our equipment halfway across the parking lot. We meekly went to a nearby small faucet and cleaned our gear.

After getting everything clean we went back to the motel and went to bed immediately. We were all kinda tired. Maybe Jason will look at a map the next time he schedules us at a rodeo so far from home – but I doubt it. That's all right, though. We all had fun at Auxvasse.

At 8 a.m. the next morning we left for Tunica, and it wasn't really a big deal getting there. We drove south through Missouri, across a part of Arkansas, then into Memphis, then down Highway 61 into Mississippi. Tunica is in the northern part of the Mississippi Delta, only about an hours drive from Memphis.

It was 6 p.m. when we checked into our rooms at Tunica, and the rodeo didn't start until 8 p.m., so we had some time to look around. Tunica was once a small "cotton town" but now it is known as the home of a huge gambling casino complex located on its outskirts. We went to the casino named Sam's Town, not to gamble but for two reasons: it was the host hotel for the rodeo, and we'd never been inside a real casino. It was huge. I've seen bingo halls on Seminole Indian Reservations in Florida, but they are a drop in the bucket compared to this place.

If they looked at our faces, everyone could tell it was our first time in such a casino. Our eyes were as big as silver dollars. We were amazed. We just staggered around, gawking at everything.

We finally left the casino and went to look at the arena, which turned out to be an asphalt parking lot with about 2 feet of dirt on top of it. The arena was set up around the dirt. You might think that two feet of dirt is enough cushion to keep you from being hurt if you are thrown, but remember, there's 6 inches of asphalt under that dirt. If you hit it hard enough it will smart.

Jason and I both had really good bucking bulls. Either one of us could have won the bullriding on those bulls, but unfortunately, we both got bucked off.

I was really disappointed. I said, "There goes my trip to Cheyenne."

Jason was disappointed too. We all just loaded up and headed back home.

The next weekend Greg Mc and I went to the rodeo in Marianna. As I said before, there was only $500 added, and I really needed to make some money for the Cheyenne trip. If I didn't do well, there was no hope left.

Greg Mc and I both drew good bulls. I rode my bull and scored 80 points. Greg Mc, as well as everyone else, got thrown off. I won everything: entry fees, day-money, and the pot. My winnings totaled $1200. Now I had the money for Cheyenne! I breathed a sigh of relief.

At a rodeo as small as the one in Marianna the winner might win $480 or so, but these were extenuating circumstances, all in my favor. It couldn't have happened at a better time.

Greg Mc and I had another rodeo the next weekend, the semi-annual Silver Spurs Rodeo in Kissimmee. This one was not as big as the annual Silver Spurs. I hadn't planned on this rodeo. I guess I just overlooked it, but luckily, Greg Mc entered Billy and me.

My bull at Kissimmee lost his flank rope just outside the chute, and when this happens, the judges automatically give you a re-ride – it's a rule. Well, the judges got mad because they didn't notice the violation and the chute boss and I had to point it out to them. I guess that kinda ticked them off. I was supposed to get my re-ride that day or night, but they made me wait until the next day. That wasn't right.

The other guy who went with us, Billy Carter, got a re-ride too, and he got his re-ride that night. But it almost turned out tragic. Billy's bull bucked him off, and we thought he'd broken his neck. Greg Mc and I went to the hospital with him and stayed there until he was released at midnight – really bruised and sore but unbroken.

After leaving the hospital we checked into a motel not far from the arena and crashed. The next day I got my re-ride. I rode my bull to a third place, and it paid about $300. The trip to Cheyenne was looking easier to deal with.

Finally it was the week before the Cheyenne rodeo and time to go. Tracy took me to a friend's house in Ocala to meet the Curry's and load my stuff. It was goodbye for just two weeks, but Tracy and I hadn't been apart for that long in almost 2 years. It wasn't as easy to say goodbye to her as I made it seem in front of Jason and the others. Maybe I was just trying to appear too "manly."

Sorry Tracy.

Chapter 34

The
Trip
to
Cheyenne

When you're rodeoing hard you drive a lot at night. Although you pass through lots of pretty scenery you don't get to see much of it. This trip would be different.

We left for Cheyenne a week before the rodeo was scheduled to begin. There were five of us: Mr. and Mrs. Curry (Jason's parents), Jason, Shell, and myself. The Curry's rented a mini-van for the trip. Mrs. Curry said she had saved lots of money for a really nice vacation, and this would be it – not just a trip to a rodeo.

I took $800 with me, plus I would write a check for my $300 entry-fees. Mrs. Curry paid for a lot of stuff along the way.

We didn't even attempt to take the most direct route to Wyoming. Instead, we went wherever Mr. and Mrs. Curry wanted to go. If I took a map of the United States and traced our route on it, it would look like the path of a drunken sailor.

We went through Alabama, Mississippi, Louisiana, Arkansas, Oklahoma, the panhandle of Texas, through Wyoming, and up to Montana.

We drove mostly during the day, so we saw much of what those states have to offer. We saw the cotton fields of Mississippi and the great Mississippi River, which I had passed over at least ten times but almost always at night. We saw some of the bayou country of Louisiana. We stopped in a little town there to eat and had some genuine Cajun cooking. I don't know the name of what I ordered, but it was pork – or "pok" if you're Cajun – and it was great!

This little town had an old district with some of the original houses dating back into the last century, and Mrs. Curry wanted to see it. We stopped at a convenience store and I went inside to ask the clerk where it was. After I asked the man behind the counter for directions, and he started talking, I couldn't believe my ears. He was a Cajun – I mean a real Cajun – and I couldn't understand one word he was saying. I just nodded my head and smiled.

When I came back to the van Mrs. Curry said, "Are we close?"

I said, "I don't even know where I am right now."

Needless to say, she looked at me kinda funny.

We did eventually find the place, and the old houses were beautiful. After a couple of hours there we bid a fond farewell to Cajun country.

We headed into Arkansas and passed through the western side of the Ouachita Mountains and the southern tip of the Ozarks. Somewhere along the way we stopped at a little country store kinda like a mom and pop grocery. We stopped for gas and for cold drinks and snacks. There was a bench on the front porch of the store, and four or five local men were sitting there. They really stared at us, as if saying, "Ya'll don't belong here. Best move along."

We did. As soon as we got our gas we found the next road heading to Oklahoma. Later, we all laughed about it. They were probably "pulling our leg," and it worked.

Once we got into Oklahoma we went through Henryetta and then stopped for the night in Shawnee. By the way, we had stopped twice before, and we would always get a double bedroom and a fold-up bed for me. I can tell you for sure that those fold-up beds are the most uncomfortable things in the world to sleep on. Not much better than a hay rack with a little hay spread on it.

After breakfast the next morning we headed out again, through Tulsa and then down into Texas. We weren't in Texas very long, but we did stop in Amarillo for a couple of hours. We found a discount boot outlet there. I didn't buy any boots, but I did buy a nice cowboy shirt. It was red and black checkered on the yoke and one sleeve, and white everywhere else. It was kinda flashy, and I looked forward to wearing it for Tracy.

When we left Amarillo we drove through New Mexico and then to Pueblo, Colorado where we spent the night. The next morning we wanted to do a little sightseeing, but we didn't know where to go. We drove around until we found an information center. Mrs. Curry went inside and came out about an hour later with our plan.

We first drove out of Pueblo, our destination being the Royal Gorge. The approach to it is a tourist spot. There is an old western frontier town where you can watch gunfights or just hang around the saloon. They also have wagon rides and horseback riding and an old steam engine train that takes you to the canyon.

We all rode the train first. We did get close to the canyon, but we would get even closer later on. After the ride we watched a couple of gunfights, had a beer in the saloon, and took a wagon ride, then we headed for the main attraction, the Gorge.

On the drive to the canyon there were a couple of

deer standing beside the road. I don't know what kind they were, but they still had velvet on their horns. We stopped, and I got out of the van first. I was snacking on peanut butter cookies, and I offered some to the deer. They loved those little cookies and ate them right out of my hand. I thought that was great. The closest I had ever been to a deer in Florida was on my plate or at Silver Springs in Ocala. I've never been into deer hunting, and a wild Florida deer certainly won't eat out of your hand. I've seen plenty of them on the prairie and in hammocks, and they will run if you get within a hundred yards of them.

Jason and Shell got out and started feeding them too, but not before Shell got a picture of me feeding them. Then every car coming along stopped, and everyone was feeding the deer. More and more deer were showing up for the handout. You can see antelope almost everywhere in Colorado, Wyoming and Montana, but you'd never get this close to them.

We finally left and drove on to the Gorge, and the view was breathtaking. This canyon was formed by the Arkansas River, and it is also called "The Grand Canyon of the Arkansas." The walls are a 1,000 feet tall, and they stretch for 10 miles. It is awesome. Standing there, gazing at this thing formed by nature alone over such a long period of time, without the help of bulldozers or draglines, makes you suddenly feel small, no matter if you are 5'4" or 10' tall.

There is a bridge across the canyon, and it is the world's highest suspension bridge. We didn't drive across it as others were doing, but we did walk out to the middle, and that was enough for all of us. It must have been 1,500 feet or more from that bridge down to the river, and that's a long way straight down. To tell the truth, it scared the heck out of me, and I didn't stay there long.

There is a train track running along the canyon wall next to the river, and it appeared to be dangerously close to the river. I'm pretty sure it's not for commercial use. We could also see rafters below, and they looked like corks bobbing along the swift water.

It was about 6:30 when we left the Royal Gorge and went back to Pueblo for the night. The next morning, after we all got dressed and had breakfast, it was already 94 degrees and it was only 10:30. We left for our destination, Ft. Collins, Colorado where we would stay for the week of the rodeo.

Ft. Collins is only a 35 or 40 minute drive from Cheyenne, and that's as close as we could get rooms. That's how big this rodeo is. Hotels and motels in Cheyenne, and for miles around, are booked months in advance.

As we were leaving Pueblo we decided not to take the direct route to Ft. Collins but to drive up through the Rocky Mountains. We just ambled along, enjoying the sights. The antelope were everywhere, and the mountain scenery was spectacular.

We stopped in a little mountain town about 2:30 for a late lunch, and when we got out of the van it was 55 or 60 degrees. We couldn't believe it. Just a short time before we were hot as heck, and now we were cold. I've seen 55 degree and colder weather in Florida every winter, but there's nowhere in Florida where you can drive for an hour or more and experience a 40-degree drop in the temperature. That's rough on a Cracker.

The hometown people in that little restaurant looked at us as if we were kinda crazy because we were all bundled up in jackets. To them it was normal summer weather, but to us it was cold.

After lunch we took the most direct route we could find to Ft. Collins, and we checked into our motel about 9 p.m. Even with all the sightseeing and stops along the way we were four days early when we arrived there on Wednesday. The rodeo started at 2 p.m. Monday and continued until the next Sunday. Jason and I were up Monday and Friday. Cheyenne is a 3-header, but you only get that 3rd bull if you ride the first two and score well enough so those two scores add up high enough to be in the top 15 for the rodeo.

Ft. Collins is a college town, the home of Colorado State University. Since I live only about 25 miles from Gainesville and the University of Florida, I am a little more familiar with that kind of town than the other places we passed through. Familiar except for one thing: at about 9 p.m. in Ft. Collins they close down one or two city blocks for pedestrian use only, students or otherwise. I guess this was one of the main streets because we'd leave our motel at 7 p.m. to eat in one of the downtown restaurants, and on the way back we would have to detour a pretty good way around that street to get back to the motel. In Gainesville, they don't close down the main city street for students or anyone. Walk out there at 9 p.m. and you'll get creamed. Maybe Ft. Collins has a better idea.

The next morning Mrs. Curry had a good idea: she wanted all of us to go whitewater rafting. It was a good idea except I didn't want to go! I'd seen that stuff on TV, and it looked dangerous. I don't mean I'm scared of water – I'm scared of drowning in it. I didn't let anyone know my feelings on this so we drove to a shop that sold all kinds of rafting equipment: canoes, wet suits, kayaks, and anything else some one would need. For the inexperienced, they also ran guided whitewater rafting trips.

While Mrs. Curry was asking about the guided trips I was hanging back, just looking around the shop. I figured she'd sign up her family and Shell. If I wanted to go I'd have to pay for it myself, which I had no intention of doing. I thought I'd just spend a quiet day at the motel, but I was wrong.

I'd already gone back out to the van when all of them came out. They were all happy to be going on this great adventure the next day. I was happy too because I thought I had dodged the bullet. Then Mrs. Curry turned to me and said, "I signed you up too."

I didn't know what to say. I couldn't say, "There's no

way in hell you're going to get me on that river!" So I just said, "Thank you." I tried to think of a way to get out of it, but there was no way.

After an almost sleepless night the dreaded day came. We were to meet the buses at 10 a.m. at a Jiffy store 5 miles out of town.

The tour managers who met us there had wet suits for rent. I'd been told back at the motel that the water is really cold, about 56 degrees, so I rented one. Jason and all the others started making fun of me. I said, "When we get on that water we'll see who's laughing and who's freezing their butts off."

They decided I was right, and the wet suit wasn't a bad idea, so they rented suits too.

There were two buses, and both of them were booked full. We got in one bus, and off we went into the mountains. We drove five or 6 miles and then stopped in a small parking lot. The rafts were on trailers hooked to the busses. We unloaded them, carried them down to the river, and waited.

Shortly after that the guides came down and gave us instructions, such as how to paddle and how to get back in the boat if you're thrown out. There would be only six people to a boat, which worked out fine for us because there were five of us and the guide would make six.

Our guide was a girl – or woman – in her mid-twenties, but it was evident she knew what she was doing. Having a female guide was fine with me because a male guide might try all that macho B.S., and I was in no state of mind to put up with that. If we had drawn a male macho showoff there might have been a fistfight between us when the trip ended.

As we started to get into the boat I asked if I could be in the left front because I thought I could paddle better on that side. The guide said, "Sure, but you'll have to listen to me carefully as we move along. You'll be the lead rower, and everyone has to follow your rowing rhythm. Just be sure you follow my instructions."

I said, "I guess I'll give it a try. I just hope we don't wreck because of me."

Before the water became rough and took all of our attention, the guide told us that this river is called "Cache La Poudre River." It was named that because back in the days when settlers were crossing the mountains a group of them got caught here in a winter storm. Their barrels of gun powder were so heavy they bogged the wagons down in the snow, so to keep the powder from the Indians they hid the barrels in the high banking walls of the river. That was quite a history lesson, but I was more concerned about the rapids.

We were moving fast now, and the scenery was beautiful. We had already hit two bad spots where the water got pretty rough. After we came out of the second set of rapids the guide said, "That was nothing. The worst one is ahead."

That made me feel really good.

Just then we hit a medium rock and the guide was thrown out of the boat. We all panicked for several seconds because we knew we couldn't make it the rest of the way without her. We immediately turned the boat sideways so she would have a larger target, but there was a bridge right ahead. We slammed into the bridge on our left side, just behind me. That's bad, because the boat will flip over if everyone doesn't do what they are supposed to do. Mr. Curry, who was on the right side, jumped over to my side to keep my side from coming up and flipping us.

We got off the bridge in time to catch our guide. She hit the side of the boat just like we'd planned, but she went under the boat. There was rope webbing under the boat, so she grabbed that and pulled herself back up, then Mr. Curry grabbed her and pulled her into the boat. She was a little shook up, but fine.

We stopped after every rough rapid so everyone could rest, including the guide. When we stopped I'd get out and hold the boat still. The water was very cold, but pure. I'd get a good drink each time we stopped.

The funniest thing that happened on the trip – at least to me – was when the guide kept yelling at Jason to follow me, and he kept messing up. Several times she threatened to stop the boat and put him out on the bank.

When we got to the point where the trip ended, I had worked harder and laughed more than all of them, and I think I had more fun than any of them. I certainly had more fun that I'd expected.

For the next three days we didn't do much of anything. We spent our time in the motel hot tub, watching TV, and generally being lazy. It had been an exciting but tiring trip, and we wanted to rest up before the rodeo.

We left Ft. Collins early Monday morning and headed to Cheyenne. As soon as we reached the rodeo grounds we paid our fees and got our back numbers. A lot of rodeos use the back number system, but this back number had to stay intact all week. At other rodeos it doesn't matter after you've ridden once. The back number is the only pass for us to get back behind the bucking chutes, and that's the place we had to be.

I'm not real proud to say this, but I fell off my first bull. When I say I fell off, that's a way of saying the bull bucked so weakly that I kinda got disgusted and relaxed. I should have ridden that bull easily, but I just slid off and hit the ground.

On the other hand, Jason had a really good bull, but he got bucked off too. To say we were disappointed is putting it mildly. We had really looked forward to riding well, but it just didn't happen. We were determined to do better Friday.

After we got back to the motel in Ft. Collins that evening Mrs. Curry had another idea. She said, "Why don't we drive up to Montana and see the Little Big Horn?"

This time I thought this was a good idea, and so did everyone else. We made plans to leave after breakfast the next morning.

We left Ft. Collins Tuesday morning and just took our time, not even trying to reach Montana that same day. We saw a lot of interesting scenery, then we stopped for the night when we reached Buffalo, Wyoming. It seemed to be a fairly small town, but the motel there had three king size beds in each room. It was great to sleep on a real bed again.

Wednesday morning we had breakfast at a little restaurant across the street from the motel, then we drove to the Montana border, which was only an hour away, then on to Little Big Horn, about a 30 or 40 minute drive.

We reached the Custer Battlefield National Monument at 9:30 and had a little wait. When the park opened at 10 we drove in, parked and walked to the entrance where there was a museum displaying old treaties, guns, bows and arrows, pictures, and other things from that era.

There was a place down from the museum where they had displays of a typical soldier's equipment, such as a tent, sleeping roll, canteen, rifle, ammunition, and his uniform. There was also a display of Indian things: a teepee, bear skin blankets, a bow, and some arrows.

The biggest difference to me between the white soldier and the Indian was not the gun versus the bow and arrows but in the way they lived. The Indian teepee was waterproof, but the soldier's tent wasn't because it was made of what appeared to be burlap. The Indian blanket was a bear skin, and the soldier's bed roll also looked like burlap, so it couldn't have been very warm on a cold night. The Indian was dry and warm, and the soldier was wet and cold, so it seems to me that if there hadn't been so many soldiers – not to mention the white man killing all of those buffalo and causing the Indians to starve – the Indians would have kicked the white man's butt all over the West. Anyway, that's my opinion.

After looking at all the displays, we walked up the hill to Custer's grave. There were a lot of other graves there, but his had a steel fence around it and a much bigger headstone.

We walked around for a couple more hours, seeing everything there was to see, then we got into the van and headed back to Buffalo. I have to admit it was interesting to see this place, but it wasn't very exciting.

It was about 4:30 when we reached the motel where we would again spend the night. There was plenty of daylight left, so we asked the motel clerk if there was anything special there to see. He told us there was a tourist place up in the mountains just a little way out of town, so we decided to go there.

It turned out the place was mostly for campers, but they did have horseback rides. Now, Jason and I had ridden horses all our lives, and the prospect of riding a horse wasn't exciting; but being from Florida, all the riding we had done was on flat, flat ground, and this was a chance to ride the high ground. We all decided to take a ride.

When we reached a cabin where the rides started, all the horses and the guide were out with a group and would be back in an hour. To kill time, we walked up the road and came to a little café. We all went inside to look around.

Just inside the front door there was a long counter with stools, so we all sat down. Mr. and Mrs. Curry ordered apple pie, and Shell ordered a diet Coke. Shell is so petite I don't know why she'd order anything diet, but I guess most women are like that.

There was an opening to the left of us, so Jason and I

checked it out. It was a room made up to look like a rustic lodge, with deer heads mounted all around and a moose head over the fireplace. There were also bear skins on the walls.

Jason and I sat down at a table made out of a ring of wood cut from the middle of a tree. I don't know what kind of wood it was, but it was at least 3 feet or more wide. There was a checker/chess board painted on the wood, and this was glassed over with shellac.

We got the checkers from a waitress and started playing. We weren't really keeping score on who won the most games – we just had fun.

After about an hour we left for the horseback rides, but when we got there they were closed for the day, so we went back to the motel. The next morning we packed up, ate breakfast, and drove all the way back to Ft. Collins.

Friday morning it was back to the rodeo, this time with anticipation of good rides. Unfortunately, it turned out to be an exact repeat of Monday. I drew a bull that didn't buck well, and Jason drew one that really bucked. We both ended up in the dirt.

After every ride you try to put a period after that episode and correct what you did wrong, and that's what we hoped to do. Sometimes one bull isn't enough to work out the bugs. Jason and I both had some bugs, but we couldn't work them out. We had looked forward to riding well and winning some money, but again it didn't happen. We were disappointed, but all the fun we had took our minds off this and eased the pain of failure.

We drove back to Ft. Collins and spent the night, then the next morning, Saturday, we headed east out of Colorado. We drove to Lincoln, Nebraska and spent the night, and after that, the only stops we made were for gas and food.

It was 3 p.m. Monday when they dropped me off at

my house, then they all headed on to Clewiston. During the trip I spent all of my $800, and counting my $300 entrance fee, I was out $1100 with not a dime of winnings, but to me, it was worth every cent. During my lifetime I have been to many rodeos, some of them far away, but this trip to Cheyenne was a highlight, one that will remain in my memory forever. As I was to learn in coming years, if you don't have pleasant memories to fall back on, you have nothing.

This was also the last rodeo I went to with Jason. It wasn't because we had a falling out with each other or anything like that; it's just the way things worked out. Jason wanted to go to some rodeos I didn't want to go to, and other rodeos we had to go to on different days because of our schedules.

I guess you could say this was the end of the "Jason and Pee Wee" era of my life. It was fun ... every step of the way.

Odessa, FL., 1995. Pee Wee riding Mission Impossible. Photo: Mike Rastelli

Chapter 35

**Back
to
Greg
Mc**

Conyers, GA., 1995. Pee Wee placed 4th with a 72 point ride on this 5 Star Rodeo Company bull named Mountain Man. Photo: Mike Rastelli

Greg Mc and I started traveling together again. Over the next two months, August and September, we entered and went to six rodeos: Crossett, Arkansas; Jonesville, Louisiana; Lauderdale, Mississippi; Conyers, Georgia; Adel, Georgia; and Memphis.

We'd entered Crossett for Friday night but had to leave for Arkansas Thursday after work. I had taken a lot of days off of work at the door-mill to go to rodeos, and the boss was very aggravated by it. When I told him I wanted Friday off, he said, "If you take one more day off, you're fired."

I thought about it for a moment, then I said, "Well, consider Thursday my last day here."

I'd enjoyed working there but I couldn't stand the owner. He wasn't very nice to anyone. I was having fun rodeoing, and I was winning enough money to get by, so I just said to heck with it.

It was our plan to leave Thursday evening and drive straight through to Mark's house (Greg Mc's brother) in Monticello, Arkansas, and go on to the rodeo from there. Greg Mc would take first turn at the wheel and drive to Mobile, then I would drive on from there.

When we reached Mobile I was so groggy I said to Greg Mc, "I'm too tired to drive. Pull over and let's get some sleep."

Greg Mc agreed. He pulled the car as far as he could off the road, and we both went to sleep. The next thing we knew it was daylight. We were only a block from a Burger King, so after getting some breakfast, I took the wheel. We didn't stop again, except for gas, until we got to Mark's house at 2:30 p.m. that afternoon.

The rodeo didn't start until 8 p.m., and Crossett wasn't but about 30 miles from Monticello, so I went with Greg Mc to see some Monticello friends he hadn't seen in a long time. We first went to a feed store, then to a beauty parlor. I don't know who he was visiting or why. The only thing I remember was that the folks at the feed store were older than us, and mostly younger at the beauty parlor.

We got back to Mark's at 5:30 and got ready to go to the rodeo. As he always did when we came up there, Mark went with us, and we enjoyed his company. We arrived at the rodeo arena just a little past 6:30, paid our fees, and went behind the bucking chutes. Then we got a surprise – there were girls back there! We weren't used to this at all.

The main reason we weren't used to this is that when the guys gather behind the chutes, they change from the pants they're wearing into their "riding pants" – so there we stood with our britches off, and those girls didn't give us even a second glance.

We soon learned that the girls were there because, at this rodeo, they were having women's bullriding. This was unusual, almost unheard of. There is an association for women, and I think it's called W.P.R.A. – Women's

Professional Rodeo Association – and they do ride bulls and bucking horses. They do almost everything men do in the P.R.C.A., but the events are almost never combined at the same rodeo. I guess the committee wanted to see how women riding bulls would go over with the crowd.

The women don't ride bulls that buck as hard as the ones we get on, but their bulls are pretty bucky and put on a good show. There were eight girls there to ride. One of them came up to me and asked if I would pull her rope for her when her time came. I was so surprised I just stammered for a moment, then I said yes.

Now, I don't mind saying that this girl was very cute. She had long brown hair, a pretty face, and everything else – if you know what I mean. I couldn't see the color of her eyes. I did pull her rope, and out of the eight girls, she was the only one to make a qualified ride. I felt pretty good about this.

Then it was our turn. My bull was supposed to really buck, and he did buck pretty good, but not good enough. I rode him and scored 76 points, but right then 80 was winning the last paying hole. Greg Mc had a really good bull, better than mine, but he got bucked off. At least I got some day-money, so I couldn't complain.

After I'd packed up my gear that pretty little bullrider came up and asked if I was going to the rodeo party they were having in town. Lord knows, I was tempted, but I said, "No, I'm going with my traveling partner back to his brother's place in Monticello."

We could have gone, but all three of us would have been in deep trouble if we had stayed up there partying all night. We drove straight back to Monticello.

The next morning Greg Mc and I ate breakfast with Mark and his family, said our goodbyes, and drove straight back to Florida.

The next weekend Greg Mc and I entered rodeos in

Jonesville, Louisiana for Friday night and Lauderdale, Mississippi for Saturday night. We left for Jonesville Thursday afternoon after Greg Mc got off work. Remember, I'd quit my job the week before. Greg Mc couldn't afford to do this because he had a family to support.

We again drove all night but it wasn't as far as we thought, and we got to Jonesville about 9 a.m. We went straight to the rodeo arena just to get a look at the place and see our bulls. I'd drawn a bull that was new, so I wanted to find him and see what he looked like. I wanted to know him when he came into the chute that night so I could put my rope on him and be ready when my turn came. Greg Mc drew a bull we both knew, so he was just helping me look for mine.

When we found my bull Greg Mc and I kinda laughed. He was a slab-sided Brahman crossed with something else – I couldn't really tell what it was. He didn't have the big Brahman hump but he did have thin skin like a Brahman, and he had short horns about 4 inches long. He wasn't much to look at.

We had a lot of time to kill until 8 p.m., so we went to a restaurant to eat. After lunch we played the slot machines. Just about every place in Louisiana has those things. We got bored pretty quick, so we drove around town.

We came across a little bar with a pool table, so we decided to go inside and play a few games. When we walked in and ordered two Cokes and no liquor, the bartender was kinda surprised, but he was friendly. We played three or four games, then we sat down at a table, drinking our Cokes. Two locals came in and ordered beers, then they started playing pool. They were friendly too. They smiled and said hello. Seems we always ran into friendly people in Louisiana. No one ever gave us a hard time because we were "Florida Cracker" cowboys.

We finally left the bar and went back to the rodeo grounds to get some rest in the car. At 8 p.m. Greg Mc and

I started getting ready. The bullriding was the last event, so we had plenty of time.

When my time came they ran my bull into the chute and he was even more skinny than I thought – that's what "slab-sided" means. When I had my rope pulled tight I nodded. When he came out he went two jumps, then he spun to the left, but the poor thing was spinning flat, not kicking up at all. I said to myself, "Man, I could really give this bull a spur bath."

But I didn't. I guess I felt kinda sorry for him, so I just sat in the middle and rode him to the whistle.

After I'd gotten off and away from him, all I could do was laugh. Every bullrider there – including me – knew that this bull had no business in a P.R.C.A. rodeo.

Greg Mc's bull threw him off. We both knew that his bull was very hard to ride, but I thought Greg Mc could ride him.

After we packed everything in the car we headed east to Lauderdale, Mississippi, which is close to Meridian. I knew in advance I had drawn a bad bull at this rodeo. He was the kind of bull that really tries to jerk a rider down on his head. That kind of bull can rearrange your face. I'd seen him buck several times, and he always did the same thing: he jerked the rope out of the bullrider's hand because the rider was concentrating on not getting jerked down. I'd never seen him ridden for 8 seconds, and I knew if I could ride him I'd have a good score.

Greg Mc had drawn a pretty good bull too, so we were both hot to get there. We drove straight through and arrived at the rodeo grounds at 12 noon – way too early again. The rodeo didn't start until 8 p.m.

We had to find something to do to kill time. It was really hot, so we went to Wal-Mart, not to go shopping, but to get out of the heat. We stayed in that place for at least 3 hours, then we went back to the rodeo grounds.

As we walked to the arena we got a real surprise – there stood Jason and Shell! We all sat around shooting the bull until it was time to go behind the chutes and get ready.

My bull was a big brindle with short horns. When I say big, I mean he was over 1,800 pounds. Well, I had my game plan on how to ride him. I kinda had a knack for riding bulls like him, ones that we call "jerk down artists."

Greg Mc and I always pulled each others rope when we could, so Greg Mc pulled my rope. I slid up and got a good seat, then I nodded. That bull really blew out of the chute, then he bucked toward the fence just like I thought he would. He was trying to jerk me down, but I was hanging tight. When he'd almost reached the fence he turned hard to the right, and when he did, he jerked my rope completely out of my hand. I'd already pitched my left hand free and turned my head and upper body to the right, trying to make the corner. When I did this I dropped off in the well – that's what we call the inside of a bull's spin. Instead of just hitting the ground, I landed on his head. That's when trouble really started. He hooked me straight up in the air.

Things happened so fast I didn't see any of it for the first few seconds, but Greg Mc told me this later: I went about 10 feet up into the air. While I was up there, the bull stopped and waited for me to come back down. When I did, I came down back first. My body folded around his head backwards. This time he threw me 10 feet straight ahead of him.

This much I do remember: When I landed I got to my hands and knees as quickly as possible and started crawling. Now I'm sure you're thinking, why didn't you get up and run, dummy? Well, I didn't have time. Things were happening in split seconds. That bull was coming right at me for more. You'd be surprised how fast you can crawl when your life is in danger or if you're facing a lot of pain. Anyway, as I crawled away I let the bull get as close to me as I could, then I turned left so he'd run by me. As he ran by he stepped on my left foot and twisted my ankle and knee. That really hurt. I got up on my feet fast, but I couldn't put much weight on my left leg. I hopped to the fence as quickly as possible and flipped myself over to the other side. Then I just lay there for a few minutes.

When I finally got up and limped back to the bucking chute, I watched Greg Mc get bucked off too, but he was all right. I still wasn't sure I was. I also watched Jason get bucked off. I said to myself, "Man, this just isn't the Florida boys' day at a rodeo!"

Greg Mc and I packed up for the trip home, but I needed to keep ice on my knee. I knew I wouldn't be any help driving, but we got a lucky break. There was a guy there from Chiefland, Darrell, who had ridden up with someone else who was not going straight home. He needed to get back fast, so we had a second driver. I didn't have to drive at all.

On the way home my knee hurt so badly I decided I wouldn't enter the rodeo in Conyers the next weekend, but Greg Mc's wife, Janie, had already entered me. I didn't find this out until we got back from Lauderdale. In fact, I didn't know until the Tuesday before the rodeo.

I was really pissed! I hadn't asked her to enter me. I sat around the rest of the week debating if I should go and take a chance with my knee like this, or if I should call and turn-out. In rodeo language, turn-out means cancel. If you enter a rodeo and turn-out before the bulls are drawn, you don't have to pay the entry fees; but if you turn-out after the bulls are drawn, you do have to pay the fees. In this case, the bulls had been drawn, so if I turned-out I would have to pay the fees. At the last minute I decided to go.

It was so "last minute" that Greg Mc had already left with someone else. I had to go by myself in my little truck. Although Conyers is only a four and a half-hour drive, it seemed much longer while driving alone.

When I got there it was raining – not hard, just a steady mist, but everything was soaked. As I pulled in the gate I saw a beautiful sight, at least to me: a Justin Sports Medicine trailer. I knew they could help my knee. Those guys can put you back together with tape and Ace bandages.

The only dry place there was a stock trailer behind the chutes, and that's where all of the rough-stock riders were gathered. The bareback riders, saddle-broncs and bullriders all use rosin, and it has to be kept dry. After I'd hung up my rope and put rosin on it, I went to the Justin trailer. The doctor there taped my knee real good. When I walked out of that trailer I felt like I had a new knee. It felt so good I jogged all the way back to the chutes.

The bull I had drawn was one I'd been on before, and I knew he spun to the left, which would be into that bad knee, but my knee felt so good I wasn't worried. This bull was another big brindle, but he didn't have horns.

When the bullriding started it stopped raining. That was good – we didn't have to worry about the rosin getting wet. I got down on my bull and someone pulled my rope, then I took my wrap, slid up, and nodded. When the gate opened I got a surprise. The bull immediately started spinning to the right. That turned out to be a good thing. That left knee that felt so good gave out on me immediately. I couldn't hold on with my left leg at all. The only thing keeping me on was the moves I made with my free hand and my upper body, and the hold I had with my right spur.

I made the ride and ended up winning fourth place which paid over $200, so I didn't waste my money by either turning-out or getting bucked off. Everything worked out fine although I'd had lots of doubts. And I didn't have to drive home by myself. A friend who had ridden up with Greg Mc rode back with me.

Chapter 36

A
New
Job
I
Really
Enjoyed

A couple of weeks after I quit my job at the door-mill a friend of mine from Chiefland, David Carter, called and asked if I wanted to come to work for him. I said sure. Well, it turned out I wasn't exactly working for him – more like with him, or under him.

The job was supposed to be just mowing with a big tractor and a bat wing mower. This place was a big beef cattle operation, and in just a few days I was already back to doing a job I loved – helping work the cattle. They did need someone to mow the pastures, but David knew I knew my way around cattle and horses, so I ended up working cattle more than I did mowing. I loved every minute of it.

We were doing it all, including pushing cattle from one pasture to another. Sometimes this meant pushing them down a dirt road for a mile or so, and sometimes the pasture we'd push them to would be only one pasture over.

We were also penning cattle to work them, doing everything from de-worming and de-liceing them to throwing calves, castrating the bull calves, and branding and vaccinating all of the calves. We even had to rope some yearling calves out in the pasture because they were missed during the round up, and they had to go to market.

It was great except for one time. We were hauling some dairy cattle from one place to another. They'd put me in a one-ton truck to do some of the hauling, but they didn't tell me this truck had bad brakes. There I was, with a fully loaded trailer and coming up to Highway 27, when suddenly I found out the brakes weren't good. I barely got that thing stopped before I shot across 27, and Highway 27 is a very busy road. It would have been a bad wreck, maybe a disaster. After that I was more careful.

This job also wasn't in conflict with my rodeo activities. David knew I rodeoed on many weekends, including Fridays, and it didn't matter.

I really loved this job and everything I was doing. I came to realize that rodeo is a sideline, something I would surely have to quit someday as age catches up with me; but I could ride the range forever. This is the one thing I wanted to do as a life-long occupation: tend cattle.

I wish this job could have lasted longer, but what was soon to come at Brighton took care of that and much, much more.

Chapter 37

Final
Rodeo
Trip
Before
Brighton

It was the 3rd weekend in September when Greg Mc and I entered the last two rodeos we'd go to before the Southeastern Circuit Finals in November: Adel, Georgia, and Memphis. We did enter Bonifay in October, but a hurricane ripped up through the Florida Panhandle and the rodeo there was postponed until the next year.

Greg Mc and I left for Adel Saturday afternoon. Two cowboys who were on their way back from a rodeo down south had stopped and spent the night with Greg Mc, and they were catching a ride with us to Adel. Some rodeo cowboys do that – they catch rides from rodeo to rodeo with other cowboys going that way. That's just the way rodeo cowboys are. You help someone else out if you can. Another guy named Shawn, who was a friend of ours from Ocala, went with us just to help drive and pull our bull ropes.

I drove to Adel, which is just north of Valdosta, and it was only a little over 3 hours. When we were about 100

166 The Last Ride

yards from the rodeo grounds, and in sight of it, one of the guys who had ridden up with us said, "Hey, Pee Wee, you want to pull over and let me drive some?"

After we'd all had a good laugh, I said, "No, I think I'll just take 'er on in from here."

That's just an example of the camaraderie cowboys share.

The bull I had drawn was another big brindle, and I knew he was a good one, but the bull Greg Mc had was the best bucking bull at the rodeo.

I hate to say this – and I hated it even more when it happened – but it was two jumps and a thump for me. In rodeo language, that means my bull threw me off very fast. I didn't even get started riding him good before I hit the ground.

Greg Mc's bull really bucked. As soon as they opened the gate he started spinning to the left. I mean immediately! Greg Mc was making a hell of a ride, but the bull finally won. Greg Mc hit the dirt before the whistle. He got up and said, "Oh, well."

That's about all you can say when you know you tried your best. Of course some people, including myself, have used other words of the 4-letter kind to express frustration.

Greg Mc, Shawn and I headed from Adel to Memphis that night, but instead of driving half way and stopping we drove all the way and arrived there about 9:30 a.m. The rodeo didn't start until 2 p.m.

This time it was easy to find the rodeo grounds and get in. We drove all the way to the building and didn't have to park so far away and walk such a long distance as we did the last time we were here.

Everything was the same about Memphis this year – the fair and the big screen to watch the replays – but there was one thing different: we had to get on two bulls back to back. Any time you have to do this it's hard on you, mentally and physically. Well, actually, it's only hard on you if you get bucked off the first bull.

I was in a bad situation. I knew only one of the two bulls I'd drawn, and I'd been on this bull twice before. Both times he'd bucked me off. But that wasn't the worst part. He was very hard to ride – no fun to ride – and if you did make a qualified ride on him, you couldn't score very well. In other words, you'd put out maximum effort for a minimum score. The other bull was a very small red bull with no horns, and I didn't know anything about him. Another bullrider told me that he spun to the right really fast.

When the bullriding started I got set on my first bull and nodded, but he threw me off again – pretty quick, I might add. There was no time to sulk. I had to get back to the chute where my second bull was waiting. Then I got a good look at him there in the chute. He was smaller than I thought. He might have weighed 1,000 pounds soaking wet. I don't like small bulls, although I am small myself, but even if you don't like something you've still got to try your best. I put my rope on him and had Shawn pull it for me, then I slid up and nodded.

That little bull took two jumps straight out and then started spinning to the right. After about three or four rounds he somehow got me to the outside of the spin, then the next thing I knew I was under him. He got on top of me with his head and commenced mauling me. In this case, mauling means he was slinging up and down, mashing me and blowing slobber and snot all over me. Sometimes when he'd sling his head up he'd hit me in the face and head. Fortunately, he didn't knock me out or break any bones in my face.

Usually there are two or three bullfighters – or rodeo clowns – on hand to help a bullrider out in a situation like this, but this time there was only one, and he couldn't help me. The bull wasn't interested in him or anything he was doing. All he wanted was me.

Well, the bullfighter did get his attention long enough for me to get up on my feet, but as soon as I did the bull turned back towards me. I tried to run, but my left knee gave out again. There I was, being mauled again.

Finally, that little bull either got tired or bored or both. He just ran to the let-out gate.

All of this happened in a time frame of about 40 to 60 seconds. That might not sound like very long, but believe me, it felt like 40 to 60 minutes.

Anyway, Greg Mc got bucked off of both his bulls too. We both had to go home dejected. I was also a little sore.

Chapter 38

**The End &
The Beginning**

**My Life
Changes
Forever**

November 11, 1995 Brighton.
Pee Wee on V8, his last ride.
Photo: Mike Rastelli

You already know what happened to me on November 11, 1995 at Brighton, so I won't repeat all of the details. Some of it is still vivid in my mind. I remember Greg Mc rushing to me as I lay on the ground, and I remember saying to him, "I think my neck is broken." I didn't know just how "broken" I was.

There are some things about that night you don't know yet. When they flew me out in the helicopter, our destination was Tampa General Hospital in Tampa where they have one of the state's outstanding spinal cord programs and some of the best neurosurgeons. As we approached Tampa there was a bad thunder storm over the city and we were diverted south to a hospital in Ft. Myers. To put it delicately, the hospital in Ft. Myers wasn't really equipped to handle my case. Meaning – I don't think the knowledge was there.

When I got in the emergency room they did x-rays and an MRI and told me my spinal cord was severed, but what I haven't told you yet is that I had feeling down to just above my nipples, and I could move my shoulders.

That night, although I wasn't in pain, they put me on some kind of pain killers which kept me almost completely knocked out for more than two weeks. They just kept pumping them into me.

Also that same night, Tracy got to the hospital just after they'd given me the news. Then they told her. As they were taking me out of the emergency room up to the intensive care unit, I made them stop so I could ask Tracy to call my mom and dad and tell them too. I also said, "Tracy, I love you."

That's about all I remember for the next two weeks, except waking up and not being able to talk. Tracy later explained to me that they'd done a tracheotomy and a bronchoscopy because I had a little pneumonia; but after they'd done the bronchoscopy, instead of capping off the trachea and let me continue breathing on my own – as I was doing – they hooked me up to a breathing machine called a ventilator.

Remember that storm over Tampa? Well, the next time you hear the saying, "The Lord works in mysterious ways," you might want to give it a little more thought.

While I was in the hospital in Ft. Myers, lots of people came to visit me, mostly people I'd rodeoed with at one time or another. Others were just friends and family.

I'd been in the hospital in Ft. Myers for over two weeks when I was moved to a specialty hospital in Jacksonville where they were supposed to do two things. First, get the pneumonia out of my lung. They never did get it out at Ft. Myers. Second, try to get me off the ventilator.

What they did was teach me how to talk with a pas'mer valve. I couldn't talk because the trac has a balloon – the technical term is cuff – and it's blown up with air, which means no air can get to my vocal cords. When the balloon or cuff is down with no air in it, air can travel through my vocal cords, but not very much does because the air isn't forced enough. The pas'mer valve is placed onto my breathing hose so when the cuff is down I can speak more clearly, and the breath the machine gives me lasts longer because the pas'mer valve is a kind of one way valve. It lets air go to my lungs and holds it there until I let it out. When the cuff in my throat is blown up and the pas'mer valve is removed, the air still goes to my lungs, but instead of going out through my mouth and nose, there's an exhalation valve in the breathing hose that allows the carbondioxide to get out of my lungs before the next breath comes.

One night while I was in Jacksonville someone made my breathing hose too long and the exhalation valve was too far from me. Every time the ventilator gave me a breath it was forcing carbon dioxide back into my lungs because the carbon dioxide didn't have time to reach the exhalation valve before the ventilator gave me another breath. In other words, I was being poisoned. My mind was so messed up that they asked me questions I knew the answer to but I couldn't answer them. Tracy was standing beside my bed when someone pointed to her and asked me who she is. Tracy and I had been engaged for more than a year, but when I looked at her I said, "I have no idea."

That's when they jerked the breathing hose off and put on the ambou bag, which is nothing more than a bubble that can be attached to the trachea. When someone squeezes it, it gives you air. As soon as they did that my mind was clear as a bell. The hose was fixed and put back on me.

The hospital experience was terrible for me, but it would have been much, much worse except for two people: Tracy and my mom. Mom stayed at the Ronald McDonald house in Jacksonville. She came to the hospital every morning and stayed until 4 or 5 in the evening. Then – and this is the amazing part to me – after her classes ended each day, Tracy would drive from Gainesville all the way to Jacksonville just to sit with me for a few hours. That is a long drive. Then she'd drive to Callahan, which is about 35 or 40 miles west of Jacksonville, and spend the night with friends there. The next day she'd drive back to Gainesville, attend classes, then come back to Jacksonville. She did this every day for almost three months.

I did have a few visitors during my stay in Jacksonville: Greg Mc, David and Billy Carter, Jason and now Shell Curry, Bill and Cookie Morton, Dough Henry, and a guy I'd met only two months before my accident, Don Hunter. It's kinda strange because even though I didn't know him that well, Don is one of only nine or ten people who still come to see me. He asks my advice on riding bulls, like what to do when a bull makes a certain move, or something to that effect.

Also, while I was in the hospital, some rodeo friends of mine got together and put on a benefit rodeo for me in January at the Williston arena. A few of the people involved were Joey Ashin, Gene Carter, Billy Carter, Rusty Willis, and many more I'm sure. Those are the only names I know of. To everyone who was involved, from the contestants to the spectators, I thank you from the bottom of my heart. The money that was raised provided me with a van with a wheelchair lift, and it also buys most of my medical supplies.

In late February I was released from the hospital, and I was glad to be home, but before long I was back in another hospital. In early March I went to my lung doctor in Gainesville. He took an x-ray of my lungs and told me I still had pneumonia, and he sent me to the hospital where he works. I was mad that I had to go back into a hospital so soon, but the pneumonia had to be cured. I was there for eight days, and every day for six days he did a bronchoscopy, and he got it out.

I'll explain a bronchoscopy: it's a small tube with a small light attached to the tube. The tube is attached to a machine that sucks. They remove my breathing tube to go down through my trac to my lungs. The machine works like the one a dentist puts in your mouth to suck the saliva out of your mouth. Since I can't cough everyday at home, my mom does the same thing, but the suction tube we use is just a clear plastic tube. It doesn't have a camera or anything like that. She just has to go down and use the "search and find" method. I can feel my lungs, so I tell her if she's in the left or right lung. Also, I can't swallow anything, so I constantly have to have my mouth suctioned out to get out the saliva. The only way I eat is through a tube in my stomach.

Well, enough about that medical stuff. March through part of May, Tracy was doing her internship at Williston High School, and she lived here in the house with us. Her bed was almost right next to mine. At that time, the only way to suction the saliva out of my mouth was with a machine that could stay on only a few minutes at a time. Someone had to turn the machine on and off, and put the suction tube in my mouth. Tracy had to keep getting up during the night to do this, and she didn't get much sleep – not to mention all the other things she did for me.

Every day my mom, dad, brother and sister-in-law would get me up in my wheelchair, and some days Mom and Dad would put me in my wheelchair-accessible van and drive me to the agricultural building so I could take Tracy her lunch. I really enjoyed doing this.

In mid-May, not long before her graduation from the University of Florida, Tracy moved back in with her parents. My brother and sister-in-law took me to her graduation in Gainesville, and I remember feeling so proud of her. I couldn't stand the fact that I couldn't clap, whistle and holler for her when she walked up to get her diploma – cheer for her like she'd done for me so many times at rodeos.

As soon as she got her diploma I had to leave. I just couldn't stand it. I couldn't stand myself being this way.

About a week after her graduation, in June, Tracy came to my house and told me things just weren't working, and couldn't work out between us. I thought for a couple of seconds and said, "You've got to do what you feel is best for you."

She froze for a moment, and I could tell she was hurting; then she turned and left. It was over.

You don't have to feel too sorry for Tracy, though. She got a job teaching agriculture at a Central Florida high school. About three months later she was engaged to someone else, so she wasn't too heartbroken. Now she's married and happy.

Things kinda went the other way with me. I got depressed about Tracy. I stopped getting up in my wheelchair every day. I'd only get up when I had to go to the doctor or something like that. I also hated myself, hated being just a vegetable unable to do anything for myself, always dependent on others. I stayed in this deep depression for several months.

In February of 1997 my cousin Tammie and her son came down from Virginia. Tammie isn't the kind of person anyone can stay depressed around for long. In only a couple of days she had me back to my old personality. I was making jokes about everything, just the way I used to do. She pulled me out of that funk in no time flat.

Tammie had come to help Mom with me and my care. She stayed for three months, then she and her son went back to Virginia. She will never know just how much she did for me.

Something else happened in February. An old high school rodeo buddy of mine – his name is Levi – came to see me. He asked if there was anything he could do or get for me. I said, "Yes. I'd like to somehow get a voice activated computer." I'd heard about them through Tracy, and I wanted to try one.

Well, Levi organized his first benefit rodeo for me in San Antonio, Florida in the summer of '97, and it was hot!

Along with the rodeo they had an auction, which they also had at my first benefit rodeo in Williston. People donated things like shirts and hats signed by World Champion bullriders Charlie Sampson, Tuff Hedeman, Jerome Davis, and other good bullriders. There were also knives, porcelain dolls, blankets, and many other things.

This wasn't a complete rodeo. There was no bareback riding, saddle bronc riding, steer wrestling, or calf roping. There was just team roping, barrel racing, and bullriding. There were plenty of team ropers and barrel racers, but only eight bullriders showed up because there were two P.R.C.A. rodeos that same weekend.

For the eight who did show up it wouldn't be easy. Silver Spurs from Kissimmee brought some of their best bulls. Since there were only eight riders, they had to get on two bulls each. For a while it was raining bullriders. I mean they were getting bucked off right and left. It was a sight to see! Almost like a circus. But a couple of guys did ride two bulls successfully.

The second benefit rodeo was in January '98 at the Williston arena. Everything was in the same order except this time there were a lot more contestants in bullriding. Gene and David Carter provided the bulls. A lot of bullriders hit the ground, but there were some professionals like Greg Mc, Jason, Don Hunter and others, so the competition was better between the bullriders as well as the bulls.

During the time between benefit rodeos, all I could do was watch TV and stare at the ceiling. Since I am totally paralyzed, I could not do simple things for myself that others take for granted. You can't imagine how frustrating this is. I could not turn on the TV. I had to ask Mom to do this for me. I could not change channels. If a program lasted 30 minutes, and I wanted to watch something else, Mom would have to channel surf for me. If I wanted to listen to the radio I'd have to ask her to turn it on, change stations, then turn it off. If I wanted to listen to a CD, it was the same thing. If I could just get that computer things would be different for me, and I let Levi know this every time we spoke to each other.

The monotony of my life was somewhat broken when Michelle Traylor from the Williston Public Library, and her sister Kandrice Anderson, started coming out to the house and reading to me. One of the books they read was the novel *A Land Remembered* by Patrick Smith (of Merritt Island, Florida), which is the story of Florida pioneers and their love of horses, cattle and the land. I related to this. When Mr. Smith came to Williston to give a lecture, Michelle brought him out to my house for a visit. We kept in contact, and there were other visits, and this eventually led to my writing this book. If Michelle had not brought that one particular novel to read to me, Mr. Smith and I would have never met. Again the old saying, "The Lord works in mysterious ways."

Levi and his friends put on a third benefit rodeo for me, again at the Williston arena. This time he used an amateur rodeo stock-contractor who knew me from '85 because I'd been going to his rodeos since then. The rodeo was again a success because of the number of contestants and spectators. By the way, Williston people are some of the best rodeo fans around, and I'd like to thank them for that. (There would be a 4th benefit rodeo for me in Williston, February 5-6, '99.)

All those benefit rodeos finally raised enough money for me to pursue that dream. In April '98 we made an appointment to go to Tampa for a demonstration of a multimedia Max system. The demonstration was at Tampa General Hospital. The man demonstrating it was also a quadriplegic but he wasn't on a ventilator. He could use his arms but not his hands. We had been there about an hour when I asked him, "Should I get one of these? I've never had any contact with a computer. Do you think I could learn?"

He cut me off quickly and said, "If I were you, I'd want one yesterday."

So it was settled. Levi called the man who invented the multimedia Max system, Dan Degnan, and ordered it. The computer arrived at my house in May, and Dan installed it on May 11th. As far as I'm concerned, Dan and his invention are a Godsend. It has totally changed my life.

The computer itself is a Gateway 2000, but with the multimedia Max hooked into it, the computer becomes totally voice commandable. The keyboard and hand mouse can still be used, but I can do everything a person who can use their arms and hands can do – just with my voice commands. I can turn on the TV, radio, and CD player myself, by voice commands. I can turn on the lights. I've got internet access. I can even make my own phone calls whenever I want, and that's another thing Mom had to do for me.

There is one thing I can do with my voice that can't be done with the keyboard – I can dictate my words rather than having to type each letter. That's how this book was written. As a matter of fact, these words never left a computer until Patrick Smith's daughter, Jane, printed them out for him.

To explain: After dictating several pages into the computer, I would send them by e-mail to Jane, who also lives on Merritt Island. Her dad doesn't have a computer. Jane would print them out and take them to him, then he would do all the necessary editing and revisions to put the material into book form. I guess you could call it an electronic team effort, Pee Wee to Jane to Patrick. A modern day marvel. Without the computer, this book would have never been written. Mr. Smith would not have been able to sit here with me month after month after month, taking notes. And I cannot type.

Thanks, Jane. I know I ran you ragged delivering all that material. And Thanks, Patrick Smith, for encouraging me during all those times I faltered.

Now, this kinda ends my story. I went to lots of rodeos

I didn't put into the book because I didn't want to give anyone an overdose of rodeos. I've also done my share of bad things I didn't mention, things I'm not proud of. We all make mistakes, especially when we're young and carefree and think we're indestructible.

If you've enjoyed this book, I'm glad, but if you haven't, I'm sorry. This book is just about some of the places I've been, some of the things I've seen and done, and some of the people I've met and been around.

In short, I guess these are my memories, and that's all they are now. I'll never be able to get on a horse again and go riding out through the woods and prairies, rounding up cattle. I'll never again get in a car and drive a 100 miles an hour just to get to a rodeo, get on a bucking bull, and maybe ride him and maybe not, then get back into the car and head to another rodeo.

I'll never do a lot of things again, but I believe God has kept me here for a reason, even though I don't know what that reason is. I'm going to keep looking. Maybe I'll find it sooner or later.

Hey, I know there's got to be a reason. I've had too many chances to die. According to the doctors in Ft. Myers, I should have been dead within three days of my arrival there. And don't forget, I had pneumonia for four months.

God must want me here for a reason.

EPILOGUE

Sometimes when I lie here in this bed alone, just staring at the ceiling, a kaleidascope of characters parade through my mind's eye: Greg Mc and Jason and all my old rodeo buddies and many, many more people. I see all of them, and I am once again with each of them. I can also see the crowds in arena bleachers, cheering when I do well and throw my hat high into the air, and moaning when I don't do well. I can smell the odor of horses and bulls and the cold sweat coming from the riders as they await their turns.

At other times I am out on the prairie, racing Black, cutting cattle with Daddy, chasing a wayward bull or cow and forcing it back into the herd.

All of these things come back to me, forming the flow of my life, and I am lost in these images, transported back to a time when I was young and carefree and mobile and filled with life and adventure and hope for the future.

These things sustain me now, giving me hope during those times when there is no hope, silently believing that someday the medical profession will find a cure, or if not that, just make me better.

Maybe this will happen, and maybe it won't. I may remain trapped in an immobile body with my memories and dreams.

We'll see.
GOD BLESS ALL OF YOU
Glen "Pee Wee" Mercer
E-mail: MaxnPW@aol.com
18851 S. E. 11th Place
Williston, FL 32696

I was told this tale when I was 7 years old, and I have remembered it all these years. Perhaps it is symbolic of all rodeo cowboys. I thought I would share it with you.

THE COWBOY

There he sat, an old man of 37. He was a rodeo cowboy most of his life. He was also a very good cowhand, but all the broken bones had left him almost crippled. The arthritis in his joints was so painful he wasn't able to do the things he used to do.

One day he was sitting with his Jack & Coke, and it was dusk. He heard some noises outside in his old practice arena, so he went out to investigate. When he reached the arena it was dark, then all of a sudden, the lights came on.

When his eyes adjusted to the bright lights, he said to himself, "Those lights haven't worked in 5 years." Then he looked to the right, and the chutes were loaded with horses and bulls. Also, a bunch of old rodeo cowboys were standing there. He asked them what was going on, and one of them said, "We're here for the rodeo."

He was puzzled, and he didn't know what they were

talking about. They started the rodeo, first with the bareback bronc riding. All of a sudden his arthritis didn't hurt anymore, so he joined in. He rode bareback broncs like he used to. He roped calves in record times. He dogged steers. He roped steers like never before. Then it was time for the bullriding.

He was a very good bullrider, but the bulls were what crippled him up. The other cowboys told him it would be all right, but he was still a little scared. He climbed over the chute gate and looked down at the bull. It was the great bucking bull, Red Rock. He had only been ridden by one man, Lane Frost, but Lane was dead.

He got down on Red Rock, pulled his rope and said, "Outside!" He rode what seemed like an eternity, but he rode Red Rock to the 8-second whistle. The cowboys all congratulated him. But just then the sun started to rise. What he hadn't remembered was that Red Rock was dead too. The cowboys started fading, then everything started fading, including him. He said, "What's going on?"

One of the old cowboys said, "We hope you've enjoyed tonight, but now it's time to come with us."

"What do you mean?" he asked.

The old cowboy said, "Haven't you noticed that you don't hurt anymore?"

"Yes, I noticed," Old-At-37 said. "Why did this happen? I don't understand any of this."

The old cowboy then said, "When you heard the noises out here it was still daylight, but didn't you think it was strange that it was dark when you got here? It's only 50 feet from your cabin door to the arena. You're dead, son. We've come to take you home."

A
Special
Note
To
Readers

I first met Glen "Pee Wee" Mercer in the latter part of 1997 when I had a speaking engagement with the Friends of the Library in Williston. My host for the day, Michelle Traylor, took me to his house out in the country to meet him. This was before he acquired his voice activated computer, and his condition saddened me. All he could do to pass the time was lie in his hospital bed and watch television, listen to the radio, or stare at the ceiling. Also by then, many of his former friends – not all, but some – did not visit him anymore. Perhaps it was too painful for them to see him like this, and they wanted to remember him as he once was. Whatever the reason, he felt that some of his friends had deserted him.

We kept in touch, and on September 14, 1998 I received this letter: "I'm just writing you to see how you've been. I'm doing alright I guess. I got a computer, and it has opened up a whole new world for me. I can dictate things to it, as well as other things it will do for me. Mr. Smith, your book 'A Land Remembered' was such a great book I wanted to ask you a favor. I want to write my own book. But I don't know how. If you could tell me how, or show me how, or something, I would really appreciate that. I don't have any ideas what I want to write about, and I don't know where to start. I need to know how to write correctly first, don't I? If you have time, please help me. Thank you. Your friend, Glen 'Pee Wee' Mercer."

At that time I was really tied up with speaking engagements, but two days before Christmas Eve, 1998, I sat down beside Pee Wee's bed and told him he should write about himself. We discussed what we needed to do to produce this book. We began that day, and it eventually took seven months to complete.

There were many times when dredging up memories became painful for PeeWee – telling tales of things he once did and can never do again. He would become depressed and talk of quitting. When this happened, I would always not just encourage him to go forward, but insist on this. He had too much to tell to just quit.

During the time we worked together, a deep bond of friendship formed between us, and I admire him tremendously. He is truly a "Profile in Courage." I'm not sure I would have such courage in a similar situation. Few would.

Working with Pee Wee on this book has been one of the most gratifying experiences of my lifetime. Sometimes the greatest gift you can receive in life is helping someone less fortunate than yourself. I will always remember with pleasure the road Pee Wee and I have traveled together.

— Patrick Smith